Chaucer's Gardens
and the Language of Convention

Chaucer's Gardens
and the
Language of Convention

Laura L. Howes

University Press of Florida

Gainesville Tallahassee Tampa Boca Raton
Pensacola Orlando Miami Jacksonville

Copyright 1997 by the Board of Regents of the State of Florida
Printed in the United States of America on acid-free paper
All rights reserved

02 01 00 99 98 97   6 5 4 3 2 1

Library of Congress Cataloging-in-Publication Data
Howes, Laura L.
Chaucer's gardens and the language of
convention / Laura L. Howes.
p.cm.
Includes bibliographical references and index.
ISBN 0-8130-1506-5 (alk. paper)
1. Chaucer, Geoffrey, d. 1400—Criticism and interpretation. 2. Gardens in literature. 3. Convention (Philosophy) in literature. 4. Chaucer, Geoffrey, d. 1400—Technique. 5. Description (Rhetoric). 6. Rhetoric, Medieval. 7. Gardens, Medieval. I. Title.
PR1933.G37H69   1997
821'.1—dc21   97-16839

The University Press of Florida is the scholarly publishing
agency for the State University System of Florida, comprised
of Florida A & M University, Florida Atlantic University, Florida
International University, Florida State University, University of Central
Florida, University of Florida, University of North Florida, University
of South Florida, and University of West Florida.

University Press of Florida
15 Northwest 15th Street
Gainesville, FL 32611
http://nersp.nerdc.ufl.edu/~upf

To Mary and Charlie

Contents

Preface ix
Introduction 1

—— 1 ——
Gardens Chaucer Knew 15

—— 2 ——
Convention and the Poet
in Two Early Dream-Poems 35

—— 3 ——
Troilus and Criseyde:
A *Paradys d'Amours* Lost 64

—— 4 ——
Gendered Paradises
in *The Canterbury Tales* 83

Notes 111
Bibliography 125
Index 137

Preface

Chaucer's adaptation and translation of received narratives, from the French *dits amoureux* to Boccaccio's *Filostrato* and many others, has long involved Chaucerians in extensive analyses of changes Chaucer wrought on these narratives and of how he adapted the stories to fit his own culture, time, and motives for storytelling. His use of conventional *topoi*, however, has not received the same kind of attention, and has most often prompted critics to assert that Chaucer, like all medieval poets, used conventional images throughout his poetry, thereby replicating medieval commonplaces. But even with these smaller units of inherited poetic material—sometimes consisting of just a few lines in a poem—Chaucer also radically transformed what he took from earlier writers, either by modifying the inherited *topos* itself in a way that draws attention to its obtrusive presence in a text or by placing the received *topos* into a narrative context that undermines or otherwise challenges its efficacy or its conventional meaning.

Chaucer uses gardens contextually in several ways: as enclosures that delineate insiders from outsiders, as in the *Canterbury Tales* where men build enclosed gardens for women and women rail against them; as a signal of a potent love convention, as in *Troilus and Criseyde*, which then allows Chaucer to expose the deficiencies of that same convention; and as markers of a young poet's acquiescence to the poetic convention of his predecessors, as in the *Book of the Duchess* and the *Parliament of Fowls*. In all of these cases, Chaucer explores constraints imposed by conventions—both social and literary—and appears to conclude that convention is a necessary aspect of human experience and expression, though in many cases deeply flawed. For Chaucer also represents, or makes a place for, the worlds that exist outside these gardens. In the *Canterbury Tales* that feature gardens prominently, the excluded realm of female experience and desire nevertheless finds expression in Emelye's complaint, in May's subversion of January's power, and in Dorigen's realization of her predicament. In *Troilus and Criseyde*, the social realities of family bonds and military strategy, excluded from the pleasure garden, nevertheless prevail as they move from the margins of that poem to its center. And in Chaucer's early dream-poems, the poet's experience, represented by his reading and dreams, excluded from the garden in its undistilled form, nevertheless serves to demonstrate dramatically how a poet must transform raw experience as he creates a finished work.

This study explores the way in which Chaucer's garden descriptions function within several literary and cultural contexts. Discussion of gardens Chaucer knew from books he read, and of the significance of gardens to late medieval culture, contributes to an assessment of Chaucer's narrative art that reveals a deep-seated ambivalence about the role of convention per se. While addressed mainly to Chaucerians, to literary scholars of the medieval period generally, and to students, this study may also interest garden historians and Renaissance scholars investigating earlier uses of garden *topoi*.

I wish to thank first and foremost Robert W. Hanning, who listened to the kernel of this idea many years ago and saw its potential. Anyone who is lucky enough to be his student knows of his great generosity and literary acumen. Joan M. Ferrante, Sandra Pierson Prior, Christopher Baswell, and Renate Blumenfeld-Kosinski also read with great care an earlier version of this book as a Columbia University dissertation. Others who may not recall useful comments they made at various stages of this project include, most notably, William Askins, H. Marshall Leicester, Jr., and David Lawton. Bob Hanning, Michael A. Calabrese, and B. J. Leggett all read parts of this manuscript with unusual solicitude as I prepared it for publication. D. Allen Carroll, John H. Fisher, and Thomas J. Heffernan read the entire manuscript, and the work is better as a result of their insightful suggestions. For their good humor and ongoing support I am also indebted to Nancy Goslee, Mary Papke, Norman Sanders, and Joseph Trahern.

At the University Press of Florida, Jenny Brown and Deidre Bryan have seen this manuscript through its incarnations with alacrity, and the two anonymous readers for the press, who responded to my argument with just the right amount of skepticism and belief, have my unwavering gratitude. I also thank Joyce E. Salisbury and Garland Publishing for permission to reprint in chapter 2 part of my essay "Cultured Nature in Chaucer's Early Dream-Poems," originally published in *The Medieval World of Nature*. Generous research support has come from the University of Tennessee English Department's John C. Hodges Fund and from the University of Tennessee's Professional Development Awards Program. I also gratefully acknowledge the assistance of the University's SARIF Exhibit, Performance, and Publication Expense Fund for procuring photographs and photographic permissions for this book.

Finally, my parents, Raymond and Mary Howes, and my brother, Paul Howes, have cheered me on, as always. My husband, Charles Biggs, has supported me and my work in innumerable ways every single day, not least in the way that he is a present and loving father to our daughter, Mary Biggs, who was born in the midst of this project. I could not have done this without them.

Introduction

Inhabited space transcends geometric space.
Gaston Bachelard

The public and private spaces that we create—domesticated and arranged according to our individual taste and income—also influence us. When we feel the power of transcendent ideals at the entrance to a cathedral, a capitol building, or a grand hotel lobby, we sense the effects of ideas made concrete in the world. Surely we express ourselves to a degree in our spaces and in those shared with others, but the spaces we inhabit also define us, telling us not only where we are, but also who we are or who we want to be. This domesticating impulse has also influenced outdoor spaces, and wealthy men and women frequently have extended their aesthetic visions beyond the walls of their homes and public buildings onto the surrounding land. To harvest the fruitfulness of the earth is one thing; to paint, as it were, a picture of one's wealth and power with the trees, grasses, rivers, rocks, and flowers of nature is to project an image of one's position in society onto the land. Enjoying that image, then, approximates gazing into a mirror, but it is a mirror that illuminates for us how we want to be seen.

In Chaucer's *Merchant's Tale*, as many have noted, January has built for himself and his young wife May "a gardyn, walled al with stoon" (IV.2029), which joins his house and his "array" (IV.2026) in marking his status as a knight.[1] Chaucer also hints, however, that January seeks to elevate his social status with his display of wealth: "His housynge, his array, as honestly / To his degree was maked as a kynges" (IV.2026–27). The garden's stated purpose—to protect the couple's privacy during summer lovemaking (IV.2048–49)—masks only temporarily its function as an aphrodisiac for the old man, for January appears capable of several sexual acts in the garden that he cannot perform in the bedroom: "And thynges whiche that were nat doon abedde, / He in the gardyn parfourned hem and spedde" (IV.2051–52). Whereas on his wedding night, January "laboureth... til that the day gan dawe" (IV.1842), in the garden he performs and—"spedde"—he succeeds. The garden, it appears, links January's sense of himself as a man of worth to his sexual arousal and satisfaction. When performing sex in the garden he seems to draw not only on the energy of nature but also on the power generated by his own inflated, reflected image.

But, of course, no discussion of January's garden is complete without an account of May's use of that same space. And as I will discuss in chapter 4, her subversion of the paradisal matrimonial spot into a trysting place for her and her young lover Damyan demonstrates the great malleability of inhabited space, which is, after all, never entirely our own. For an individual to see in the built landscape not a mirror image of herself as she would like to be but an image of herself in thrall to another—as May is to January—can lead to subversive use of that space, to a way of commenting—by means of action in the space—on the projected image that has denigrated her.

In all of Chaucer's gardens—in the well-ordered grove of trees in the *Book of the Duchess* and in the manor gardens of *Troilus and Criseyde* and of the *Franklin's Tale*, among others—we come to know his characters by the spaces they inhabit *and* by what they do there. But because the garden comes to medieval literature laden with so many prefabricated meanings, Chaucer also represents in his gardens a whole series of subversive activities, tempered by the acknowledgment that the garden's received structure and history make such activity possible. Gardens thus provide a language of convention *and* a language in which protest can be voiced. In May's case, the garden is the instrument of her rebellion against January's tight grasp and the social conventions of medieval marriage. In other poems, Chaucer demonstrates the ambivalent nature of convention as a necessary constituent of both poetic language and social intercourse. That is, convention makes communication possible between and among poets and facilitates action in society at large. But convention also limits communication and action, excluding individuals not conversant with particular conventions, and acts as a barrier to literary and social innovation. In its capacity both to define and to limit, convention thus provides a kind of proving ground for Chaucer's relation to his poetic predecessors and as a commentary on social and cultural ideals.

It is also useful to note that some of Chaucer's fifteenth-century followers tended to reproduce Chaucerian landscapes, emphasizing their order and coherence. In *The Floure and the Leafe*, for example, the insomniac narrator, a woman, rises at three in the morning and walks "to a pleasaunt grove" (line 27) of oak trees that grow "streight as a line" (line 29) separated from each other by "eight foot or nine" (line 31), a description that recalls the grove of trees in Chaucer's *Book of the Duchess*, in which "every tree stood by hymselve / Fro other wel ten foot or twelve —" (lines 419–20).[2] Following a narrow path to "a pleasaunt herber, well ywrought" (line 49), the narrator of *The Floure and the Leafe* finds benches, newly set with turf like "green welvet" (line 53), and encircled by a thick hedge that ensures the privacy of anyone within. She thinks in such a setting that:

> There is no heart, I deme, in such dispaire,
> Ne with thoughts froward and contraire
> So overlaid, but it should soone have bote,
> If it had ones felt this savour soote.   (lines 81–84)

A soothing garden atmosphere also underlies *The Assembly of Ladies*, likewise attributed to Chaucer in the sixteenth century. This poem opens in an afternoon garden where four women walk "In crosse aleys . . . be two and two" (line 10), while others walk alone "after theyr fantasyes" (line 11), a setting and situation akin to that in *Troilus and Criseyde* when Criseyde visits with her niece Antigone in her manor garden. After an excursion into a garden maze, the narrator of *The Assembly* leaves the group by a narrow path "Whiche brought [her] to an herber feyre and grene / Made with benchis ful craftily and clene" (lines 48–49). This spot is secured "with masonry of compas environ / Ful secretly" (lines 53–54). She then falls asleep to dream of "A gentil womman metely of stature" (line 79) named Perseveraunce. As these excerpts suggest, along with the spurious attributions to Chaucer by sixteenth-century printers, Chaucer's early audiences associated him with garden settings, much as a general reader of the late twentieth century tends to identify him primarily with his bawdy tales. This study looks again at Chaucer's gardens as places in Chaucer's verse where we may discover many of the poet's main concerns.

Renaissance gardens have long been considered significant aspects of Renaissance poetry. In his seminal study *The Earthly Paradise and the Renaissance Epic*, A. Bartlett Giamatti explains: "because I think that in a garden we are at the heart of a poem and the problems it poses, I have used the gardens as images of the epics, and as means for talking about the poems as wholes."[3] Similarly, Terry Comito's *The Idea of the Garden in the Renaissance*—which had a galvanizing effect on this study at a very early stage—speaks of gardens as revelatory spaces because of "the peculiar way their forms make visible an area in which art and life, mind and nature, finally intersect." He continues: "We may thus discover in gardens models of the way in which the mind conceives its relation to the world external to itself."[4] Stanley Stewart's *The Enclosed Garden: The Tradition and the Image in Seventeenth-Century Poetry* also asserts the primacy of the garden image: "The proper context of Andrew Marvell's 'The Garden' [and several other seventeenth-century poems] is the tradition of the enclosed garden, which flourished in literary and artistic circles throughout the Middle Ages and the Renaissance."[5] Thus the garden serves as a means toward a contextual, historical understanding of certain poems, and—in an effort to chart the allusions, intellectual reverberations, and literary echoes produced in garden descriptions—scholars of the Renaissance and later periods have searched the vast history of literary gardens for guidance.

But disturbing limitations regarding medieval gardens tend to mark many Renaissance studies. Giamatti finds, because of his focus on the earthly paradise, that two traditions "develop the garden of love" in the medieval period, one being the secular tradition "which has as its site and symbol a bower or garden or grove," the other being "specifically concerned with that garden of love which is the Christian earthly paradise."[6] The myriad ways in which the garden of love is deployed in its medieval context cannot concern Giamatti. And Comito, who acknowledges that the symbolic interpretation of gardens must be informed as well by "the sorts of activity considered appropriate for gardens,"[7] nevertheless believes that "Even in the late Middle Ages, when the gardens of the *Roman de la Rose* and its progeny were flourishing in verse and floral motifs proliferated [on] tapestries, manuscripts, and cathedrals, actual gardens tended to be no more than a little green space, closed rigidly within walls or cloisters," thus restricting from his consideration a conception of the medieval built garden as a complex cultural artifact.[8] Medieval studies of the natural world have tended to take a broader view, perhaps also due to the perceived static quality of the enclosed garden, treating landscapes generally, as in Derek Pearsall and Elizabeth Salter's *Landscapes and Seasons of the Medieval World*, or symbolically, as in Paul Piehler's *The Visionary Landscape*, both of which provide extensive and insightful surveys of much medieval literature (and art, in the case of Pearsall and Salter's study). Much of what I say here is indebted—directly or indirectly—to *all* of the studies mentioned above. Their insights have consistently inspired and challenged me.

Recent work by garden historians, however, demonstrates that some medieval pleasure grounds were quite extensive, ranging in size from two to over seventy acres.[9] The small, enclosed cloister and manor garden—widely believed to be the only sort of pleasure grounds known to the medieval world—can now be seen as just one type of garden among several. As a result, some of the outdoor spaces described by Chaucer, which are not visibly enclosed or are far larger than a garden attached to a manor house could normally be, may resemble these larger pleasure grounds and not, as some critics have contended, the open wilderness. Research by Anne Hagopian van Buren on the Parc de Hesdin and Guillaume de Machaut's *Remède de Fortune*, by Michael Leslie on the landscape surrounding Bodiam Castle, Sussex, and by John H. Harvey on the archeological evidence of medieval agriculture and gardens all open the way to a new consideration of the domesticated landscape of the Middle Ages. While the enclosing wall delineating the medieval garden may remain a distinguishing feature, as Comito asserts, it is by no means its only feature, and in many instances walls enclose such a vast area that they may recede in importance the deeper one proceeds into the garden. Rather than size, then, the gardens of the Middle Ages and the Renaissance may more properly be differentiated by their placement vis-à-vis the main building. Renaissance gardens, often symmetrical, are usually situated axially adjacent to the manor house or palace, while large medieval pleasure grounds often existed at some distance from the manor house, so that part of the appeal of medieval pleasure grounds was derived from the effort involved in traveling to them.

The metaphoric resonance of gardens was firmly established by the fourteenth century. In his late-fourteenth-century ballad addressed to Chaucer, Eustache Deschamps praises the English poet's translation of the *Roman de la Rose* and his application of French genres and diction to English poetry, calling Chaucer a "Grant translateur" who cultivated an English orchard with plants imported from France:

Et un vergier, ou du plant demandas
De ceuls qui font pour eulx auctorisier,
A ja longtemps que tu edifas.

[and long since you established an orchard, and asked for plants from those who write poetry for posterity.]¹⁰

Representing the poetic process as the activity of gardening with imported plants suggests similarities between the two endeavors: they both require the manipulation of things that already exist (words and plants), and they both entail formal arrangement of those things into patterns (poems and gardens). This and other metaphorical uses of gardens demonstrate the applicability of gardening as an image for other human activities. The effort to organize, arrange, and control nature can represent metaphorically the efforts of men and women to organize, arrange, and control other forces that may seem natural, such as love or dreams.

In addition, various ways of entering or walking through a landscape can signify metaphorically acts of discovery, ways of knowing, or the experience of something new or notable. In medieval literature, the garden of love and other metaphorical landscapes often draw heavily on the notion that to walk is to know or to experience. To walk a straight path, for example, can represent the easy attainment of an ideal or love object; to follow a winding path can represent a difficult or complex experience in love. The metaphor of the path has become so common today that it has lost most of its physical or material dimension, but when Geoffrey of Vinsauf wrote about *stratum naturae*, the path of nature, as a way of organizing a narrative account,¹¹ and when Andreas Capellanus wrote of following the paths of love, their descriptions conveyed a visual and physical—perhaps almost tangible—sense of a journey through space. In Andreas Capellanus's *De Amore*, made up in large part of a series of instructive dialogues, a nobleman who is trying to persuade a noblewoman to enter into a love affair says:

Illae namque solummodo mulieres quae amoris noscuntur aggregari militiae veris apud homines laudibus dignae iudicantur et propter suam probitatem meruerunt in omnium curia nominari.... Curet ergo tantus decor tantave morum probitas amoris perambulare semitas eiusque probare fortunas. Nihil enim, quid sit vel quale, aperta potest veritate cognosci, nisi primitus illud experientiae probaverit usus. Post rei tantum experientiam decet recusare probatum.[12]

[Only the women known to have enlisted in Love's service are reckoned worthy of true praise before men, and deserve to have their names mentioned for their sterling worth in the court of mankind. . . . Therefore your great beauty and moral character should zealously traverse the paths of love, and make trial of its fortunes; for the identity and character of nothing can be ascertained openly and truly unless it is first proved by the handling of experience. It is right to reject what is on trial only after experience of it.][13]

For Andreas's nobleman, experiencing love is figured as a journey, a walk along a set of paths. Arguing that loving is like walking a path, Andreas's nobleman seeks to diminish aspects of love that might appear frightening or chaotic to the uninitiated woman. The image suggests an orderly progression of experiences that can be controlled; presumably, lovers can choose to stop loving at any time, just as pedestrians can stop walking at any moment and even retrace their steps. In addition, Andreas's nobleman argues that only in practicing love can one know love. His use of the path metaphor reinforces the notion that one must experience love before rejecting it, as well as the sense that love is an emotion that can be controlled or rejected at will. The noblewoman's retort, equally clever, also relies on a metaphorical space—the Court of Love:

In amoris curiam facillimus est inventus ingressus, sed propter imminentes amantium poenas ibi est perseverare difficile, ex ea vero propter appetibiles actus amoris impossibilis deprehenditur exitus atque durissimus. . . . Ergo talis non est curia appetenda; eius namque loci est omnino fugiendus ingressus, cuius libere non patet egressus. . . . Malo igitur aëre modico Franciae contenta adesse.[14]

[It is very easy to discover the entrance to the court of Love, yet difficult to abide there, because of the pains poised above lovers; but people find it impossible and insuperably hard to leave because of the acts of love which they crave. . . . So a court of that kind we should not approach; we should totally avoid entering a place from which it is not possible to leave freely. . . . Accordingly, I prefer to remain content within the restricted clime of France.[15]

While the nobleman claims one must walk a path to know it, the noblewoman claims that one should avoid entering a room whose doors will close and not admit release; that is, one should avoid entering into a love affair that will trap one in the painful throes of love. She thus refutes his assumption that a lover can choose to stop loving in the same way that a pedestrian can stop walking. But more to the point for this study, in both speeches, physical spaces—albeit imagined ones—serve not merely as rhetorical flourishes, images appended to an argument or narrative that could stand without them. Rather, for Andreas, the paths of love and the Court of Love serve as controlling metaphors whose images draw on the concrete reality of physical space.

Similarly, Geoffrey of Vinsauf's reliance on the path as a metaphor carries the force of physicality.

> Ordo bifurcat iter: tum limite nititur artis,
> Tum sequitur stratam naturae.   (lines 87–88)
>
> [Order can take a double road: at times it advances through the by-paths of art; at times it follows the path of nature.][16]

Order, here the grammatical subject, chooses either to follow the path of art or the path of nature. Further in the same passage, the work is said to run along the path of art ("limite currit opus" [line 91]) if its ordering of narrative events does not follow a strict chronology. Geoffrey's insistence on paths (*limes, stratum*) as useful metaphors belies—as it does in Andreas's case—a fascination with, and dependence on, the experience of a journey through space as a means toward knowledge. Geoffrey's use also implies that a journey in which choices are made can create meaning.

In fact, walking can be seen as a creative act in which the pedestrian articulates space simply by moving through it in a particular way, claiming or colonizing it for personal, private, idiosyncratic use. Any journey through space can be an act of spatial organization that not only reveals the landscape to the traveler but also offers him or her the opportunity to reorder it, as Michel de Certeau argues. Like speech acts in which users of a language system modify and appropriate that system in order to make meaning, pedestrians modify and appropriate spatial systems built to control and guide them. Writing of urban spaces specifically, de Certeau states:

> The act of walking is to the urban system what the speech act is to language or to the statements uttered. At the most elementary level, it has a triple "enunciative" function: it is a process of *appropriation* of the topographical system on the part of the pedestrian (just as the speaker appropriates and takes on the language); it is a spatial acting-out of the place (just as the speech act is an acoustic acting-out of language); and it implies *relations* among differentiated positions, that is, among pragmatic "contracts" in the form of movements (just as verbal enunciation is an "allocution," "posits another opposite" the speaker and puts contracts between interlocutors into action).[17] [emphasis original]

Just as speakers of a language do not always conform to authorized forms of their language, the urban pedestrians de Certeau describes do not conform to circumscribed, authorized pathways but instead strike out on their own across the urban landscape. Walking creates meaning, according to de Certeau; it "enunciates" a space, by tracing a path among different locations. Footsteps "weave places together."[18] A journey through space connects disparate locations into a coherent path, with each journey potentially different from every other one. Medieval writers capitalize on the association, articulated by de Certeau, between walking and creating meaning. Using travelers and pilgrims as narrators, Dante, Chaucer, and others play out two metaphorical tenors from one vehicle. Dante's journey through hell, for example, works both as a figure of his coming to know hell and its inhabitants as well as a figure of his creation—as author—of hell's geography and citizenry. Dante seems to speak in a voice backed by a higher authority, but in fact he has fashioned this version of hell, purgatory, and paradise himself.[19] Similarly, Chaucer's dream-poem narrators walk through various kinds of spaces—most of them outdoors—and thereby come to know what these spaces represent (fame, love, and so on). At the same time, Chaucer's narrators have themselves created those spaces, not by dreaming them, as Chaucer would lead us to believe, but by writing them, by making them up. At once a descriptive and a creative act, the narrated journey both describes a purported place and creates that place by means of language. Dante both describes and makes his version of hell; Chaucer both describes and makes his dream landscapes. Gardens and other landscapes in Chaucer's poetry thus serve a double function. Chaucer's landscapes become significant for what they contain, for what his characters can discover or come to realize there. They also assert the author/narrator's creative process in inventing them, since meaning derives from the choice of one garden room over another, of one path over another, of one form of knowledge or experience over others.

Further enhancing the garden's metaphorical uses in medieval literature, its importance as a medieval rhetorical *topos* deepens its significance to medieval authors and their educated audiences. Rhetorical *topoi* function as part of the language of medieval poetry, as units of meaning that hold associations with previous poems, with instances of "how and where [they are] familiarly used, or where [they have] been used brilliantly or memorably," as Ezra Pound writes of poetic diction.[20] Like the meaning of a word, the meaning of a particular *topos* is "not a set, cut-off thing like the move of a knight or pawn on a chess-board. It comes up with roots, with associations."[21] Determining the "roots" and "associations" of medieval gardens occupies part of this study of Chaucer's gardens, since determining the conventional significance of medieval gardens—both literary and built gardens—helps establish a constellation of possible meanings available to Chaucer. Among the recognizable *topoi* Chaucer knew and used are the classical *locus amoenus* and the catalogue of trees, the biblical *hortus conclusus* and the Christian earthly paradise, and the hybrid *topos* of the *paradys d'amours*. And while literary historians have constructed genealogies for these and other medieval *topoi*, they are all available simultaneously to a medieval poet. When writing, Chaucer did not need to concern himself with which *topos* had the older genealogy, which one was theoretically dependent on another. Rather, the gardens of Ovid, Virgil, Dante, Boccaccio, Guillaume de Machaut, Jean Froissart, and the Song of Songs all present themselves to him for use, their availability determined by Chaucer's own preferences and poetic needs, not by any consideration of historical primacy or the purported purity of a given *topos*.

Previous studies of Chaucer's gardens—many of them following the lead of D. W. Robertson's 1951 article, "The Doctrine of Charity in Medieval Literary Gardens"—tend to focus on Chaucer's application of a single garden *topos* and its manifestation in one or in a few poems, or they find that all *topoi* Chaucer used advance the same message against *cupiditas*.[22] But Chaucer knew of, and often worked with, several garden *topoi* and their various meanings at once, drawing on the breadth of his reading for a single stanza or image. Even when he used one text as a primary source or referent, other works he knew were potentially present for use in minor, even subversive, ways. In this manner, past works within a tradition comment on and speak to one another in Chaucer's poems. Indeed, when Chaucer's narrators walk through a particular kind of garden and describe their experiences there, the narrator has—in a metaphorical sense—entered into a past work or an inherited way of describing the landscape, and in this way he highlights his participation in an ongoing literary tradition.

Finally, this study also examines the contextual meaning of Chaucer's gardens, how his gardens function with or against the "horizon of expectations" of medieval generic conventions, in Hans Robert Jauss's phrase. With each genre within which Chaucer works come expectations about various garden *topoi*. As Jauss writes:

> The new text evokes for the reader (listener) the horizon of expectations and "rules of the game" familiar to him from earlier texts, which as such can then be varied, extended, corrected, but also transformed, crossed out, or simply reproduced.[23]

Topoi can function as part of the "rules" of a genre "game" or system and, as such, can undergo transformation as Jauss suggests. Chaucer also frequently plays the expectations generated by conventional *topoi* against a narrative environment that may thwart, parody, or criticize that same convention. In other words, the *topos* may not appear to be transformed, but in its new and inappropriate context it appears in a new light and may comment on its surrounding narrative context or may itself be undercut, parodied, criticized, or made to look artificial or nonsensical. In the discussion of Chaucer's texts that follows, the genre of each work is considered a crucial aspect of the narrative environment. In the play between contextual and conventional signification, convention emerges in Chaucer's narrative poetry as part of a malleable poetic language. Despite surface appearances—the appearance of conventionality or of a deep conservatism—Chaucer is often his most critical of established social and literary systems when he appears his most conventional.

In short, this study seeks to identify more fully than previous studies have done the literary and cultural environments for Chaucer's gardens and, by so doing, explores the way in which Chaucer's gardens function within several frameworks: metaphorical, rhetorical, cultural, and generic.[24] After a brief overview of several literary *topoi* involving gardens and ordered groves that Chaucer inherited from classical and earlier medieval authors, chapter 1 proceeds to a summary of what we know about medieval English built gardens and their role in perpetuating a medieval garden aesthetic. The second chapter initiates my analysis of Chaucer's gardens with two of his dream-poems, the *Book of the Duchess* and the *Parliament of Fowls*. The gardens in these narratives recall the tradition of garden description Chaucer inherited from medieval French poets, a tradition that Chaucer uses to address the issue of literary convention *per se* and the poet's ambivalent relation to received modes of discourse. The third chapter deals with *Troilus and Criseyde,* in which gardens and enclosed courtyards function as places where the ideal of courtly love is expressed, by Troilus twice (once via Pandarus) and by Criseyde's niece Antigone. But the ideal of courtly love, which dictates a secret love affair, also guarantees that the love of Troilus and Criseyde cannot survive the larger political forces in the poem, and in this discrepancy between the ideal and the actual lies a strong critique of courtly convention. In the *Canterbury Tales,* the subject of the fourth chapter, gardens function mainly as mechanisms of control, primarily by men over women. In the Knight's, Merchant's, and Franklin's tales, enclosed gardens represent the way in which women, as wives or as prospective wives, are treated as the property of men. As such, these gardens provide a physical and visual analogue to the filial or nuptial bonds governing female behavior. But at the same time that they express these bonds, they also afford opportunities for women to break, avert, or express their distaste for the bonds that hold and define women, as when May of the *Merchant's Tale* acquires her own key to her husband's garden gate, or when the Knight's Emelye wishes she could remain a virgin and "walken in the wodes wilde" (I.2309).

In all of these instances, Chaucer explores what it means for an individual to have to conform to conventional modes of discourse and behavior, and in each example he appears to conclude that convention must be followed—that it may be subverted or parodied, but not repealed. But his constant probing of the question, from the *Book of the Duchess,* probably completed by the time he turned thirty, to two of the *Tales* written when Chaucer was about fifty years old, suggests an ongoing investigation of the possibilities for individual expression and experience within established conventional systems—genres and *topoi,* as well as those governing social behavior.

1

Gardens Chaucer Knew

The first family of literary gardens with which Chaucer worked is distinctly French and includes Guillaume de Lorris's garden of Déduit and other versions of the *paradys d'amours* or Garden of Love created by Guillaume de Machaut, Jean Froissart, and other French authors whose works Chaucer knew intimately. A *topos* first developed by late classical authors of epithalamia, who set Venus and her attendants in a garden or bower, the French *paradys d'amours* figures prominently in two of Chaucer's early dream-poems, the *Book of the Duchess* and the *Parliament of Fowls*. Equally important, however, is Guillaume de Lorris's garden transformed and reinterpreted as a garden of sinful delights by Jean de Meun in his lengthy continuation of the *Roman de la Rose*. The garden serves as a *locus* of interpretive contention in that poem, represented at first as a place of erotic intrigue and attraction for the Dreamer/Lover; later described by Genius as a trap, a false paradise that can only lead the Lover to sin; and finally, in the poem's closing scene, as the place where the Lover consummates his passion. Compared with Genius's evocation of the "parc du champ joli" (line 19905) [the park of the lovely field], the Garden of Déduit represents the way of earthly corruption, "Ci n'a chose qui soit estable" (line 20323) [There is nothing here that can be stable], and is to be avoided by those who seek eternal life. As Genius puts it, the false paradise "cele les vis de mort anivre, / mes ceste fet les morz revivre" (lines 20595–96) [makes the living drunk with death, while this fountain (in the true paradise) makes the dead live again].[1]

Whatever Jean de Meun meant by Genius's contrast between *parc* and *jardin*, an issue still much debated, the poem as a whole provides not only "descriptions of different kinds of garden but also in the placing of those descriptions it offer[s] variety, certainty, ambiguity."[2] As Derek Pearsall and Elizabeth Salter continue: "What Geoffrey Chaucer . . . learnt from the *Roman* about gardens of paradise, heaven and hell, can partly be defined in terms of content, but more importantly in terms of complex, sometimes ironic presentation."[3] Perhaps it is this radical act of reinterpretation that compelled Chaucer to view gardens as places where meanings collide. While two of his early poems use garden *topoi* in ways that suggest their importance as recognizable *topoi* in the French tradition, gardens in *Troilus and Criseyde* and the *Canterbury Tales* dramatically challenge assumptions about their meanings, again suggesting Chaucer's indebtedness to the *Roman de la Rose* in this respect, as well as in so many others.

Both the Garden of Love and the true Paradise in the *Roman de la Rose* derive from the classical *locus amoenus*, a rhetorical *topos* first identified over fifty years ago by Ernst Robert Curtius. He argued that the *locus amoenus* "from the [Roman] Empire to the sixteenth century . . . forms the principal motif of all nature description,"[4] and he further identified its main attributes as follows:

> It is . . . a beautiful, shaded natural site. Its minimum ingredients comprise a tree (or several trees), a meadow, and a spring or brook. Birdsong and flowers may be added. The most elaborate examples also add a breeze.[5]

Curtius traces the development of the *locus amoenus* in classical literature through Homer, Theocritus, Virgil, Petronius, and Tiberianus,[6] and its importance to medieval authors may be gauged by its status "as a poetical requisite [listed] by lexicographers and writers on style,"[7] including Matthew of Vendôme, who uses an expanding description of a *locus amoenus* in his example of *amplificatio*. A small part of the exemplary poem reads:

> Flos sapit, herba viret, parit arbor, fructus abundat,
> Garrit avis, rivus mumurat, aura tepet.
> Voce placent volucres, umbra nemus, aura tempore,

Fons potu, rivus murmure, flore solum.
Gratum murmur aquae, volucrum vox consona, florum
Suavis odor, rivus frigidus, umbra tepens.   (I.111.49–54)

[Here blossom bloom
Sweetly, herbs grow vigorously, trees leaf profusely.
Fruits abound, birds chatter, streams murmur, and
The gentle air warms all. Birds please with song, groves
With shade, breezes with warmth, springs with drink, streams with
Murmuring, the earth with flowers. Pleasant is the stream's
Sound, harmonious the birdsongs, sweet the flowers, cool
The springs, warm the shade.][8]

The crucial features clearly remain shade, warm breezes, flowers in bloom, birdsong, and running water.

Tertullian, Prudentius, and other early Christian writers used similar aspects in their descriptions of the earthly paradise, transforming the classical *topos* of a perfect spot into a Christian *topos* of *the* perfect spot.[9] As A. Bartlett Giamatti puts it, "it would not be unfair to say that Christian poets plundered Elysium to decorate the earthly paradise."[10] Giamatti also notes several aspects unique to the earthly paradise: "the marvelous odor of the spot," "four rivers [which] watered the garden in Eden," and the presence of gold and jewels.[11] In the Middle English *Pearl*, for example, the earthly paradise, visited by the narrator in his dream, includes birdsong, fragrant fruit trees and herbs, and a river from whose bank he comes to see the celestial city. In addition, the *Pearl* poet decorates paradise with a path of pearls (lines 81–82), trees with silver leaves (lines 76–77), and a riverbed of gemstones, all while retaining the requisite aspects of the *locus amoenus*:

The dubbemente of þo derworth depe
Wern bonkeȝ bene of beryl bryȝt.
Swangeande swete þe water con swepe,
Wyth a rownande rourde raykande ary3t.
In þe founce þer stonden stoneȝ stepe,
As glente þurȝ glas þat glowed and gly3t,

As stremande sterneȝ, quen stroþe-men slepe,
Staren in welkyn in wynter nyȝt;
For vche a pobbel in pole þer pyȝt
Watȝ emerad, saffer, oþer gemme gente,
þat alle þe loȝe lemed of lyȝt,
So dere watȝ hit adubbement.
(lines 109–20)[12]

[The adornment of those splendid depths
Were fair banks of bright beryl.
Swirling pleasantly, the water did sweep by
With a whispering murmur, flowing straight on.
On the bottom were bright stones
(Which) shone as through glass that glowed and glinted,
As shining stars, when men of the marshlands sleep,
Stars in the heavens in a winter's night;
For every pebble in the pool placed there
Was an emerald, sapphire, or another noble gem
So that all the pool gleamed of light
So glorious was its adornment.]

Here the earthly paradise almost exceeds the poet's efforts to describe it; the poet must resort to simile, likening the pebble-gems to something his "stroþe-men" might have seen: winter stars in the night sky.[13]

Late classical authors also used the *locus amoenus* in erotic love poetry. Claudian's description of the garden of Venus in his *Epithalamium de Nuptiis Honorii Augusti* affords a good example; a place that knows only spring weather, adorned with flowers tended only by Zephyr, and home to birds Venus has chosen, the goddess's home also includes two fountains—one sweet and the other bitter—and a palace made of emeralds, beryl, jasper, and agate.[14] Statius too identifies a *locus amoenus* as the abode of Venus in his *Epithalamion in Stellam et Violentillam*, an association preserved in Isidore of Seville's incorrect etymology for *amoenus*; he believed that *amoenus* was derived from *amor*.[15] Vernacular poets, initially in Provençal and French, further applied the *topos* to love poetry. As Giamatti ascertained, "the garden of love is used throughout Provençal love poetry as the secluded, ordered, beautiful setting for the seizure by, or the loss of, love,"[16] a description that could also serve for Guillaume de Lorris's garden in the *Roman de la Rose*.

Guillaume's garden, as well as many others in medieval literature, also owes a debt to the biblical image of the enclosed garden, set forth in the Song of Songs (4:12) and taken up by writers as a *locus* for, and as a symbol of, the Virgin Mary. One of the earliest exegetes to connect the Virgin with the *sponsa* of the Song of Songs, Paschasius Radbertus, a ninth-century abbot of Corbie, compares the Virgin's purity and fertility with the beautiful enclosed garden.[17] Twelfth-century commentaries further developed the Marian reading. Rupert of Deutz explicitly links the *hortus conclusus* to the earthly paradise and further emphasizes that Mary was "*conclusa*, 'closed,' both when she conceived, and at the moment of the birth of Jesus."[18] Guillaume's use of the *hortus conclusus* demonstrates how the *topos* was readily adapted to love poetry, as were many other lines of the biblical text. In the *Roman*, the enclosure stimulates the dreamer/narrator to desire entrance into the garden, since he anticipates a state of perfection, although it is an imagined perfection very different from that alluded to by Marian lyricists and described by Christian exegetes. The *paradys d'amours*, the Garden of Love, thus combines the enclosure of the *hortus conclusus* and its attendant exclusion of the imperfect outside world with the sensuous appeal and overall sense of well-being associated with the *locus amoenus* and the Christian earthly paradise.[19]

Most of these garden *topoi* that Chaucer inherited from his medieval and classical predecessors stress positive aspects of the garden and its perfection in the service of human comfort, both physical and spiritual. But in Jean de Meun's reinterpretation of Guillaume de Lorris's Garden of Déduit, from a delightful pleasure park to a garden of sinful delights, a *hortus deliciarum*, Chaucer found a model for the garden's dark side. Not every enclosed garden guarantees pleasure to everyone who enters. Young May of the *Merchant's Tale* is more of a prisoner in January's garden than a benefactress, that is until she is able—with Damyan's help—to transform her prison into her own paradise of earthly delights. And Dorigen of the *Franklin's Tale*, whose rash promise to Aurelius is made within a garden, finds the restrictions of the promise—represented by the garden's borders of castle and sea—also prisonlike, certainly confining. In these and in other ways, Chaucer creates gardens with negative aspects, at least to some characters, and so demonstrates the power of conventional *topoi* to constrain and limit individual choice and action.

Chaucer also used the classical *topos* of the catalogue of trees, originally distinct from garden *topoi* but one that came to be associated in certain contexts with gardens. Ovid, Statius, Claudian, and Joseph of Exeter all include lists of trees in their descriptions of nature, which Chaucer probably knew.[20] Such passages, in which trees that do not naturally grow together are found side by side in an ideal landscape, are "bravura interludes," according to Curtius, "in which poets try to outdo one another."[21] They show off a poet's command of a vast vocabulary within the constraints of meter. Many such lists in epic poems define the trees by their usefulness to humans, and, in the context of the trees' being felled to make a hero's funeral pyre, their being burned stresses the wastefulness of war.[22] Other applications of the classical catalogue of trees include a list of fruit trees, most often as part of a *paradys d'amours,* stressing their fragrance and the production of food without human effort. Guillaume de Lorris's garden holds an excellent example:

> Ou vergier ot arbres domesches
> Qui charjoient e coinz e pesches,
> Chastaignes, noiz, pomes e poires,
> Nesfles, prunes blanches e noires,
> Cerises fresches vermeilletes,
> Cormes, alies e noisetes.
> De granz loriers e de hauz pins
> Refu pueplez toz li jardins,
> E d'oliviers e de ciprès
> Don il n'a guieres ici près.   (1347–56)

> [There were the domestic fruit trees, bearing quinces, peaches, nuts, chestnuts, apples, and pears, medlars, white and black plums, fresh red cherries, sorb-apples, service-berries, and hazelnuts. In addition, the whole garden was thronged with large laurels and tall pines, with olive trees and cypresses, of which there are scarcely any here.][23]

Guillaume further stresses that five or six fathoms separate each tree from its neighbors and that their branches join to form a canopy of welcome shade overhead.[24]

The significance of *topoi,* however, extends beyond their individual attributes. A *topos,* according to Quintilian, is the seat or home of argument (*argumentorum sedes*), the place where one goes looking for something to say.[25] Curtius asserts that *topoi* were "storehouses of trains of thought," and that in the postclassical period, *topoi* become rhetorical clichés that link a poet to his or her predecessors.[26] Mary Carruthers' assessment of *topoi, topica,* and commonplaces (*loci communes*) refines Curtius's definition considerably. Among other things, she stresses the physical nature of an individual's memory, and she links the idea of rhetorical commonplaces to the development of individual character: "The words *topos, sedes,* and *locus*, used in writings on logic and rhetoric as well as on mnemonics, refer fundamentally to physical locations in the brain," where memories are stored and organized for future use.[27] Further, according to Carruthers' research, each individual was expected to build up, over the course of his or her lifetime, a memorial structure, sometimes figured as an "inventoried set of bins or animal-pens, into which observations and knowledge, all experience of the world however derived, are sorted and contained."[28] These bins are the topics, or places, of memory, and what they hold makes thought possible: "whatever thoughts one has will necessarily be structured by this previously laid-out inventory of experience and will find their appropriate place, each contributing its 'bit' to the general store."[29] A commonplace, then, is a "memory-place," and as such is constituted from individual experiences, including the reading of books. But these "pieces of the public memory"—what one has been taught and what one has taken from one's experience in the world—have also been "domesticated and familiarized" by their inclusion in an individual's memory system.[30] Thus, a commonplace is not simply what one has memorized from the work of others but is what one makes of what one has gathered, and this will depend on where one has placed it, what it is next to, and what it will rub up against in that particular "bin." Finally, Carruthers emphasizes that the organizational structures of memory are "*inventional,* both in the sense of putting things away and in the sense of discovering things" (emphasis original).[31]

With this in mind, we may understand the confluence of various garden *topoi* as inevitable; that is, placed together in the same memory "bins" of countless medieval readers, gardens in classical and early Christian literature and in the Bible may easily be retrieved or considered together, their similarities and their differences noted, their conventional images put to use in any number of ways for any number of individual reasons. For Chaucer, garden description is a demonstration of his "storehouse," what he has put in it and what he retrieves from it. Garden descriptions signal his link to his poetic predecessors, but also his difference from them.

As recognizable *topoi,* gardens connect an author to those who have written before him or her, but, as a constituent of memory, they also come to represent a poet's distinct experience. The role of gardens in the world of sense perception and physical experience further contributes to their worth as poetic devices.

A description of the ideal pleasure garden written by Albertus Magnus around 1280 stipulates a turf lawn, turf benches, and seats placed "somewhere in the middle . . . so that men may sit down there to take their repose pleasurably when their senses need refreshment," trees or trained vines for shade, except in the open middle section of the garden, and a "clear fountain of water in a stone basin should be in the midst."[32] We cannot determine how much of Albertus Magnus's sense of pleasure gardens was influenced by other textual accounts (including those mentioned above as using garden *topoi*), how much was influenced by his experiences of actual gardens, and how much by tales brought back to Western Europe by crusaders and pilgrims to the Near East and Spain. But, significantly, the same features described by Albertus show up both before and after 1280 in medieval literary descriptions of gardens *and* in the records of actual grounds, suggesting the interdependence of these disciplines and the impossibility of establishing lines of influence that would point in only one direction.

Garden historians aim to establish facts about medieval gardens: their layout, the number and types of plants propagated in them, and the like. Many discount the role of literary *topoi* in the design of medieval gardens, preferring an approach that focuses on our modern conceptions of the scientific achievement of medieval botanists and herbalists.[33] But medieval garden design, the product of a culture fascinated with literary garden descriptions and with illustrations depicting gardens, necessarily contributes to, and derives much from, aesthetic concerns current in the culture at large. The history of gardens, particularly those designed for the pleasure of members of the upper class and nobility, must involve an examination of aesthetic crosscurrents, of the complex associations among texts, built gardens, paintings, and other visual arts. In at least one instance, at Henry III's Guildford manor, beginning in 1268, an English court painter directed work on an herber, suggesting a close association between painting and garden design.[34] That the descriptions of medieval garden theorists should match closely those found in literary texts, especially on the importance of shade trees, turf lawns, pleasant-smelling flowers and herbs, and the sound of running water, reinforces the notion that garden owners sought to re-create on their own spot of earth the gardens of art and literature that intrigued them. Indeed, as I will discuss below, twelfth-century romances including the *Roman de la Rose* may well have inspired the creation of the celebrated Park of Hesdin in Artois, itself the setting for Guillaume de Machaut's *Remède de Fortune;* the Tristan and Isolde story may have suggested the layout of "Rosamund's Bower" to Henry II at Woodstock; and an interest in the Arthurian legend's Lady of the Lake may be discerned at Bodiam Castle in Sussex. In addition, as Derek Pearsall and Elizabeth Salter observe: "representations of secluded garden retreats have almost as much to say to us of medieval gardening practice as of devout symbolism. We know that illustrations to Boccaccio's *Decameron* were actually used for gardening treatises, so exact and particular were some of their versions of the gardens in which ladies meditated or received their lovers."[35] Literary descriptions inspired built gardens, and illuminations from literary manuscripts could also serve as prescriptive models for gardens.

An Italian follower of Albertus Magnus, Piero de' Crescenzi, writing in Latin in 1304–1309, expands on Albertus's pleasure garden description with the addition of two sections detailing the creation of larger grounds, one discussing medium gardens of about one to four acres, and one on "the gardens of kings and other illustrious and rich lords," of twelve acres or more.[36] For medium gardens, Crescenzi suggests that such gardens be "surrounded by ditches and hedges of thorns or roses. . . . and made flat on all sides." Fruit trees (pear, apple, palm, lemon, mulberry, cherry, plum, fig, nut, almond, and quince) should be placed "twenty feet apart more or less," depending on the size of the trees, suggesting that mixed forests served as "bravura interludes" in built gardens as well as in poems.[37] Vines should be grown between the rows of trees, and "trellises and pergolas in the most suitable part [should be] made like tents or pavilions."[38] Of the largest gardens, Crescenzi recommends a

> "flat place be chosen. . . . of twenty *jugers* [12 ½ acres] or more . . . and surrounded by convenient and lofty walls; in the north part a grove of diverse trees should be planted, into which wild creatures placed in the garden may fly and hide. On the south part let a handsome palace be built, to which the king or queen may resort when they wish to escape from grave thoughts and to

refresh themselves by these joys and solaces; . . . In some part of the garden a fish pond should be made. . . . Also there should be in the garden a construction with walks and bowers made entirely of leafy trees, in which the king and queen with the barons and lords may sojourn under cover without rain. . . . The aforesaid [summer] palace may quickly be made of dry wood, and on each side round about vines may be planted to cover the entire edifice; elsewhere may be made arbors of wood or trees and covered with vines.[39]

Robert Calkins believes that both Albertus Magnus and Crescenzi "seem to be describing traditional layouts which they observed being used around them and which appear to have been in continual use into the fifteenth century."[40]

The earliest recorded royal gardens in England predate Albertus's treatise and belonged to Henry I (1100–1135), who dedicated land at Windsor Castle, at Woodstock near Oxford, and at his manor Kingsbury by Dunstable to ornamental pleasure gardens and parks. The garden at Kingsbury covered nine acres.[41] And while we do not know specifically how these early English gardens were organized, twelfth-century gardens in France of about the same size comprised enclosed, well-tended orchards with grafted trees, many containing large animals such as deer, and pools stocked with fish. According to John Harvey, Charles V of France had a pleasure garden of about twenty acres at Hôtel St. Pol in Paris, fitted out with "trellised pavilions, a labyrinth, tunnel arbours, plantations of cherry-trees and many kinds of ornamental plant." In 1398, Charles VI replanted the garden with, among other things, "115 grafts of pears . . . , 100 common apple trees . . . , 12 Paradise apples . . . , 1,000 cherry trees . . . , 150 plum trees . . . , 8 green bay trees . . . , 300 bundles of red and white roses . . . , 300 bulbs of lilies . . . , and 300 flag iris,"[42] testifying to the grand scale of the effects sought by the wealthiest men of the period.

Further, these pleasure grounds were sometimes built at a distance from the residence, so that people had to traverse land or water to get to them. By the thirteenth century, a pleasure garden at Windsor Castle existed at some distance from the castle: "In April, 1239, the bailiffs of Windsor were enjoined 'to cause our garden outside our Castle of Windsor to be enclosed with a ditch.'"[43] These instructions are followed by subsequent orders for "fencing and palings for enclosing the garden" and "a fair shrubbery" to be made in the same garden. In April 1251, a "stable for the King's and the Queen's horses 80 feet or more in length" was ordered constructed "outside the King's Castle there, near the King's garden," and in May 1256, "a well of freestone was directed to be made in the garden." A wall, first mentioned in October 1260, was finished in November 1263, suggesting that it may have been quite long.[44] In the fifteenth century, King Henry V of England built a "Pleasance" at Kenilworth Castle beyond the "Great Pool." Howard Colvin notes that "The quadrangular site was moated and there were towers at the four corners. The center was laid out as a garden, and there was a dock for boats to bring parties of courtiers on summer outings from the castle."[45] A plan of Kenilworth Castle made by John Harvey shows that a boat would need to travel the length of the Great Pool, over half a mile, to get from the Castle to the "Pleasance."[46] This distant garden was not the only garden at Kenilworth; another stood adjacent to the castle. Part of the pleasure derived from such gardens stems from the necessary movement away from the castle or manor house toward the enclosed pleasure ground, or through different and increasingly remote sections of the landscape to the farthest one, where a pavilion or smaller manor house might be discovered. The Park of Hesdin, created by Count Robert II of Artois in the late thirteenth century, consisted of three main areas, all enclosed by a wall that delineated its eleven-kilometer (or roughly seven-mile) perimeter. Anne Hagopian van Buren describes its features thus:

> Eleven gates and several posterns opened into a whole countryside of game-filled hills, pastures, and woods. . . . the southernmost [section] compris[ed] the gardens and meadows that served the castle. Here were orchards of apple, cherry, plum, and pear trees and gardens of osiers, grapevines, roses, and lilies, including one called "li petit Paradis." . . . Woods and hills filled the central section. The northern section, called "li Marés," the marsh or fen, included the valley of the Ternoise. The river and neighboring springs fed several fountains, a watercress pool, and a large fish pond, providing water for orchards, vineyards, gardens, a large stud farm, an old manor known as "li manoir dou Marés," and a building called "li paveillon dou Marés." . . . The Pavilion was the nucleus of a whole complex and larger than its name implies. It contained a kitchen and at first one and later two galleries for the

entertainment of the owners and guests who came to hunt birds in the marshes of the river shore.... The complex was surrounded by a meadow containing a fountain whose crenellated basin was surrounded by a slate-covered seat and shrubbery hedge and several gardens containing bowers or gazebos. One of these was a rose garden with a little stone tower inside, like the Castle of Jealousy in the *Roman de la Rose*.[47]

Aside from the obvious appeal of orchards and flower gardens within sight of the castle, the appeal of a well-tended private destination three kilometers from the castle, featuring all one would need for the entertainment of guests, depends in part on the experience of traversing space. Stephen Murray and James Addiss have described well the sequential experience of space at Amiens Cathedral:

The church is more than an abstract plan and physical structure: it is an experienced spatial entity. In this processional path the spaces gradually and progressively reveal themselves in a set of transformations of the initial order.... the visitor, whose movement energizes the spaces, transform[s] reality. Through his or her sense of wonder the visitor recreates the cathedral in a way that is already anticipated by the master designers, but also in a way that is peculiar to each individual.[48]

A similar sort of pleasure attends the progressive discovery of bowers, fountains, stone towers, and the like in an expansive pleasure ground, as at Hesdin. Leaving the nearer precincts at Hesdin, one would travel through the park's middle wilderness area before coming upon the marshy valley with its own series of gardens, its meadow with fountain and seats, its fish pond, manor house, and large dining pavilion with kitchen.

On the grand scale, the movement from near garden to false wilderness to far garden emphasizes the extent of the owner's holdings and his wealth. At the same time, this progression engages the traveler physically—kinesthetically—in a minijourney of discovery, analogous in some ways to religious pilgrimage. Just as the experience of walking or riding to a shrine adds force to the experience of contrition and redemption sought during pilgrimage, the physical journey through a large pleasure ground could deepen the rider's engagement with that space. That one of

Figure 1. Pleasure garden, *Le Roman de la Rose,* ca. 1485, Flemish. British Library, MS. Harley 4425, fol. 12v (detail). Reprinted by permission of the British Library.

the destinations at Hesdin was a rose garden with ties to the *Roman de la Rose* suggests that, as in so many other ways, medieval love experience could be figured as religious, a secular experience that echoed or mimicked the experience of the Divine. Further, because "footsteps weave places together" as de Certeau writes, the journey itself creates meaning.[49] The course one chooses to travel on any given day "appropriat[es] . . . the topographical system on the part of the pedestrian" (or horse-rider, I would add here). It is also "a spatial acting-out of the place . . . and it implies *relations* among differentiated positions."[50] The central "wilderness" at Hesdin contained several roads crisscrossing the area, including "li vert chemin" [the green road], "li chemin dou Roy" [the King's road], "li chemin des Bas" [the low road {which followed the Tornoise valley}], and "li chemin de Fountaine aus Dames" [the road of the fountain for ladies].[51]

On a smaller, more intimate scale, the experience of walking within these garden areas at Hesdin, discovering the various bowers, gazebos, and the "Castle of Jealousy" in the far marshy area, would similarly engage the pedestrian in a journey expressive of individual choice and desire, of individually created meaning. Such an appeal is suggested by a fifteenth-century illustration for the *Roman de la Rose*, which shows a man and woman entering a pleasure garden, the same man walking along one of its paths, and a large group gathered in a third area of the garden singing to the accompaniment of a lute (Figure 1). While this illumination emphasizes one possible passage—from the entrance at the lower right corner to the turf lawn surrounding the fountain—other choices are suggested by the pathways not followed. The section at right contains several raised beds, and some of the paths between them lead beyond the frame of the picture. The viewer glimpses one small area of a larger pleasure ground, it seems, for not only is the area at right cut off from our view, but the left boundary of the turf lawn and the nature of the space along the bottom of the picture both remain unspecified. The man depicted at the gate and walking toward the group arranged on the lawn appears to have chosen a well-traveled path, but the image illustrates that other paths were available to him as well.

Bodiam Castle in Sussex provides another example of how the sequential enjoyment of the domesticated landscape may have been fostered. Michael Leslie argues that the castle and its environs were designed as a large water park, so that anyone approaching the castle "would have begun to be aware of bodies of water surrounding him, and the castle almost swimming in its landscape."[52] An earthen mound to the north of the castle might be a "viewing terrace," with the remains of buildings at its top.[53] Visitors to the castle would most likely have been invited to stroll or ride through the landscape, to view the castle from a variety of vantage points, and to enjoy the sequential nature of their discoveries. Built by Sir Edward Dalyngrigge (also Dalingridge) from 1385, the castle and the surrounding landscape may be intended as an allusion to Arthurian legend. Leslie speculates that the "highly romantic image of a castle, perceived across a landscape, is a persistent element in Arthurian legends.... and I wonder whether there is some association in the minds of those creating these medieval landscapes between the image of the floating castle, the island fortress, and the concept of the kingdom itself."[54]

Other large pleasure grounds in England during the late Middle Ages include those at Clare Castle in Suffolk, those belonging to John of Gaunt, Chaucer's patron and friend from about 1374 on, and those of the crown. The principal gardens belonging to the king—at Eltham, Sheen, Westminster, and Windsor—all employed full-time gardeners, but the "most puzzling and intriguing of the royal gardens of medieval England," according to Howard Colvin, was at Woodstock near Oxford.[55] Called "Everswell" in the Middle Ages, the garden became known as "Rosamund's Bower" in the sixteenth century after a mistress of King Henry II (1154–1189), Rosamund Clifford, who was said to have lived in the garden within a labyrinth.[56] Colvin describes the medieval garden, which may or may not have had a maze, as dominated by water features:

> The accounts [from 1166 onwards] refer to the "larger" and "smaller" pools (*fontes*), the former surrounded by a "great cloister" (*magnum claustrum*), the latter by benches. The "cloisters round the pools" were ordered to be paved and wainscoted in 1244. By this date there was a complex of chambers complete with chapel, kitchen, and wine cellar, which made Everswell into a self-contained living unit quite separate from the royal house a few hundred yards away. In 1239 Henry III ordered an herbarium to be made round one of the pools. Another was made in 1251–52, and in 1264 Henry ordered a hundred pear trees to be planted in it.[57]

Colvin suggests that Everswell may have been inspired by Sicilian gardens, due to the many political connections between England and Sicily in the twelfth century, but he also posits a literary source, a twelfth-century version of *Tristan and Isolde*:

> In this poem the lovers were accustomed to meet in an orchard near the royal castle in which Isolde lived. This orchard was surrounded by a strong palisade, and at one end of it there was a spring from which water first filled a marble pool and then continued in a narrow channel that ran through Isolde's apartment in such a way that Tristan was able to communicate with her by

dropping twigs into the stream. Whether at Woodstock the channel actually passed through the room known as Rosamund's chamber is not clear, but the chamber and the running water were undoubtedly in close proximity. Everswell, in fact, provided the complete mise-en-scène of the poetic episode: the enclosed orchard; the spring with the stream flowing first into an artificial pool and then into a narrow channel; and the chamber or "bower"; and finally the lovers, in the persons of Henry [II] and Rosamund.[58]

"Rosamund's Bower" may thus provide another example of the influence of literature on garden design.

By the fourteenth century, some members of the lesser nobility in England appear to have followed the royal lead in the construction of large pleasure grounds. The Lady of Clare, Elizabeth de Burgh (who died in 1360 and who was the grandmother of Chaucer's first royal patron, also named Elizabeth de Burgh, Countess of Ulster), directed several improvements in her gardens, including the construction of a moat surrounding the garden, a small house in an herber built "for the Lady's deer," a glass chamber inside a pheasant house, and a "tomb" in the herber, whose function is unknown. During the years 1341–1352, new sand for the paths, new railings, new turf for repairing an area called the "Great Herber," new hedges, a bridge, and a fountain were all purchased.[59] The younger Elizabeth and her husband Lionel, Duke of Clarence, inherited the castle and grounds from Elizabeth's grandmother in 1361,[60] and another burst of repair activity is recorded for the years 1387–1388 when Roger Mortimer (the grandson of Elizabeth and Lionel by their daughter) was in residence. Gladys Thornton, in her history of Clare, Suffolk, writes of Mortimer's contributions: "the wall round the garden and the hedge round the fishpond [were] repaired . . . [and] one great lock and key was bought for the secret door of the tower."[61] From the financial records, we can understand this garden as a large area, separated into several outdoor rooms, both great and small, some housing deer, pheasants, and a fishpond, some laid with green turf. Buildings, such as the tower with a secret door, could have been used for solitary or social pleasures. Again, the experience of walking through such spaces, spotting deer and birds, and watching fish swim in the pond all would have contributed to the progressive enjoyment of these grounds.[62]

Figure 2. Illumination by "Johannes," ca. 1400, English. Bodleian Library, Oxford. MS. Bodley 264, fol. 258 (detail).

John of Gaunt also spent a great deal of his resources on castles, manor houses, and their grounds. At his Savoy Palace in London, many improvements are recorded from the 1360s until 1381, when it was destroyed in the Peasants' Revolt. The garden there, situated between the palace and the Thames, included fruit trees and a fishpond.[63] Expansions to Hertford Castle from 1372 to 1397 included a "new lodge in the old park," and Leicester Castle, one of Gaunt's favorite residences, sported a large lodge, named Birds Nest, in nearby Leicester Forest.[64] While these hunting lodges and forests may not seem relevant aesthetically to medieval garden design, they do contribute to an overall sense of aristocratic interest in land use for pleasure as well as for the display of social status. Moreover, given the elaborate arrangements for hunting parties at Hesdin, Gaunt's lodges may have been more luxurious than we now imagine them.

Pleasure grounds were not the sole province of secular lords and royalty. Many monasteries grew most or all of their own fruits and vegetables, of course, but some monastic gardens were also maintained specifically for the sick and the infirm.⁶⁵ Several influential and wealthy ecclesiastics of the later Middle Ages also enjoyed large private gardens. A double-moated garden at Peterborough Abbey, made in 1302 for Abbot Godfrey of Crowland, covered two acres and was separated from the "Derby Yard," the "Great Court," and the abbot's living quarters by a wall built in 1308. This garden was in addition to several smaller gardens and vineyards that served the abbey.⁶⁶ Also early in the fourteenth century, Winchester Cathedral Priory maintained a three-acre pleasure garden with a gazebo entrance. According to John Harvey, "In 1336 the monks, through the Archbishop of Canterbury, obtained a licence from the king to build an archway carrying a gallery . . . over the city wall . . . to reach these gardens without having to use the public road."⁶⁷ While not as extensive as the royal grounds, nor as elaborate as those of the Lady of Clare, these

Figure 3. Illustration from a manuscript of the poems of Christine de Pizan, ca. 1415, French. British Library, MS. Harley 4431, fol. 376 (detail). Reprinted by permission of the British Library.

Figure 4. Giovanni di Paolo, "Paradise," ca. 1445, Italian. Tempera on canvas, transferred from wood. 18½ x 16 inches. New York, Metropolitan Museum of Art, Rogers Fund, 1906 (06.1046). All rights reserved, Metropolitan Museum of Art.

ecclesiastical and monastic gardens nevertheless testify to the extent to which the vogue for pleasure grounds had grown in England by the time Chaucer began writing.

What were such gardens used for? In all likelihood, medieval garden activities included repose, dining, walking, and the entertainment of visitors—leisure activities that further mark these pleasure grounds with a sense of exclusivity, wealth, and privilege. Surviving illustrations of gardens from the fourteenth and fifteenth centuries frequently depict gardens as meeting places, often for lovers, but sometimes for several couples or groups of friends. Manuscript illustrations of couples in pleasure gardens include one from an English manuscript (c. 1400) depicting a king and queen seated on turf benches playing a game of chess (Figure 2). A gardener works in a wood or orchard in a separate enclosed area and both garden areas contain raised beds of flowers. A French miniature from a collection of the poems of Christine de Pizan (c. 1415) shows two lovers conversing at the edge of a turf lawn, leaning on a rose-covered trellis (Figure 3). A crenelated wall marks the far edge of this garden, and because no corners are visible in the miniature, the garden appears to be quite a bit larger than the area shown. Still, it is the intimacy of the couple—their elbows touching at the top of the rose trellis, their eyes not quite meeting—that suggests the kinds of pleasures one might expect in garden settings.

The intimacy of reunited friends is movingly portrayed by Giovanni di Paolo di Grazia (Figure 4). Dated to the middle of the fifteenth century and inspired by Dante's description of Paradise, this painting depicts the earthly paradise as a large turf lawn surrounded with fruit trees.[68] The paired figures, all locked in intense gazes of recognition and rapt attention, speak volumes about the social and intellectual pleasures associated with places of repose. And while the canvas appears rather crowded, it is also clear that the privacy of a walled garden has been achieved in this heavenly spot where no wall is visible or necessary and where language itself appears inconsequential. Other images from the period include groups of men and women dining together, dancing, and (as in Figure 1) singing.

In medieval literature, too, gardens tend to serve as meeting spots, as places where two people might hold a private conversation or a group might engage in pleasant conversation and storytelling.[69] When one person ventures into the garden alone, or separates from the group, it is most often so that he or she can then be overheard. Several medieval narrators get their material as garden eavesdroppers, including Chaucer in two of his early dream-poems.[70]

2

Convention and the Poet in Two Early Dream-Poems

The gardens in the *Book of the Duchess* and the *Parliament of Fowls* are metaphorically rich. The *Book of the Duchess,* with its version of the *paradys d'amours,* and the *Parliament of Fowls,* with its love garden that mixes versions of the *hortus conclusus, locus amoenus,* and catalogue of trees, both refer explicitly to the French court poetry Chaucer drew on for these early poems, specifically the love debates and love visions of Guillaume de Machaut and Jean Froissart, as well as the *Roman de la Rose.* But Chaucer's use of familiar garden *topoi* also refers to the entire issue of one poet's dependence on, and independence from, the poets who came before him. As R. A. Shoaf and H. Marshall Leicester, Jr., among others, have pointed out, Chaucer uses the image of an old field planted with new corn in the *Parliament of Fowls* to adduce the relationship between old books and new uses of them:

> For out of olde feldes, as men seyth,
> Cometh al this newe corn from yer to yere,
> And out of olde bokes, in good feyth,
> Cometh al this newe science that men lere. (22–25)

But while Shoaf concentrates his attention on the "violation" of the old field, the necessary plowing under that creates a fertile earth, which is analogous to the misreading of original texts he sees as central to Chaucer's work, Leicester maintains that Chaucer "affirms the *auctoritas* of received culture" with these lines.[1]

Indeed, Chaucer uses the storehouse of conventions he inherited, including those relating to the garden, to communicate with an audience familiar with poetic conventions. But at the same time as Chaucer uses conventional *topoi* and "affirms" *auctoritas*, he manages to subvert or question their efficacy, emphasizing both the uses of and the limitations to conventional language. Not only do Chaucer's early gardens raise issues of poetic inheritance and the role of conventional language, but each poem—taken as a whole—follows a pattern of narrative development that traces the poet's experience in writing from first conception to finished poem. The narrator of each poem begins slowly and diffusely, coming to the "story proper," or the "real subject," of his poem only after several hundred lines.[2] Only after the narrator has entered a garden does a coherent plot emerge; these gardens represent the narrator's acquiescence to the demands of narrative convention. Thus, the narrator's entrance into the garden—produced, of course, by his description of the garden—is also an entrance into a conventional framework that promises to give coherence to his previously unorganized account. In both poems, this promise is fulfilled, and so the pattern of preliminary narrative, entrance into the garden, and main narrative enacts the evolution of the narrator's experience in writing a poem—from preliminary, unorganized string of events to the organization of these events in a conventional manner. The garden, as a natural space that has been organized by human effort, serves as a representation of the narrator's efforts to control and organize his otherwise unruly experiences. Some critics have chosen to identify the difference between these two phases of the dream-poems as that between lyric and narrative modes, arguing that the early phase of each poem is lyric, while the central part of each poem is narrative.[3] But it seems to me that the narrator asserts his intention to tell a narrative early in each poem, although in each poem he does not tell a coherent or successful narrative until he has entered the garden.

That Chaucer's dream-poems raise such literary issues has been noted by many, and Steven Kruger's assessment of the genre helps explain why Chaucer and other authors found it so appealing:

> The dream fiction, by representing in the dream an imaginative entity like fiction itself, often becomes self-reflexive. Dream vision is especially liable to become metafiction, thematizing issues of representation and interpretation.... Framing his or her

poem as a dream, the medieval author focused attention on a human experience clearly linked to literary process, and the reader of a dream vision was prepared for a poem that, examining dream experience, might also examine its own status as poetry.[4]

In addition, in Chaucer's case, both the dream and the poem are influenced by antecedents: the dream by waking experience, the poem by the poet's experience and by his or her reading of other poems. Both are unique expressions of an individual's ability to integrate various and disparate influences. Both are by their nature subject to interpretation and reading, to misinterpretation and misreading. Further, the fact that a dream can only be communicated through language clouds the distinction between a dream and its poetic representation. While a dream-poem purports to present a dream as the dreamer experienced it, it has necessarily undergone a transformation in its retelling. It has already been interpreted once by the dreamer before it is available for further interpretation by the dreamer and his or her audience.

The *Book of the Duchess*, in many respects derivative, opens with several conventional set pieces, and as a result seems disjointed as a narrative. Nearly four decades ago, Charles Muscatine wrote that "It is difficult to distinguish the surface incoherence of dream sequence from the incoherence of plot sequence that is characteristic of conventional narrative of this kind."[5] And while more recent critics have sought to explain the poem's "surface incoherence"—or to explain it away, arguing that a medieval audience would not perceive the poem as incoherent[6]—the issue will not disappear since the narrator characterizes his own work as disjointed, acknowledging the difficulty he has in keeping to the story. Indeed, as I shall argue, in the *Book of the Duchess* Chaucer purposefully made his poem incoherent and disjointed in order to explore the relationship between literary convention and an individual poet's attempts to forge a new poem. The first 444 lines of the poem resemble a rambling account more than they do a coherent, plotted narrative, and it is not until the narrator engages the man in black to tell his story of love and of loss that the poem is transformed from a plotless account into a more conventional poetic narrative.

The garden in the *Book of the Duchess* ushers in this transformation.[7] Readily recognizable as a conventional *topos*, as are several of the other images in the poem, the garden communicates efficiently the expectation that is synchronous with such places, that is, the promise of a significant event, probably amatory in nature. The "floury grene," shaded by an orderly grove of trees, has been cited by critics as conventional, though there is no agreement on what its conventional meaning might be. A handful of critics have used their interpretations of the garden to support thematic readings of the poem, but it seems to me that the conventionality of the garden *is* its thematic meaning.[8] The garden *topos* stands for the narrator's entrance into a conventional narrative, and as an acquiescence to the conventions of writing a story.

In the first third of the narrative, the dreamer repeatedly admits that his poem does not follow a single story line, and, like several of Guillaume de Machaut's narrators, he has difficulty keeping to his "first mater."[9] At several points he passes up opportunities for elaboration and development, claiming that he must get on with his story. The issue takes shape very early in the poem: "Foor there is phisicien but oon / That may me hele; but that is don. / Passe we over untill eft; / That wil not be mot neede be left; / Our first mater is good to kepe" (39–43). In reporting Alcione's death, the narrator similarly corrects himself:

> With that hir eyen up she casteth
> And saw noght. "Allas!" quod she for sorwe,
> And deyede within the thridde morwe.
> But what she sayede more in that swow
> I may not telle yow as now;
> Hyt were to longe for to dwelle.
> My first matere I wil yow telle,
> Wherefore I have told this thyng
> Of Alcione and Seys the king.   (212–20)

The narrator claims that he will leave some things out that he could put into his story in order to get on with his "first mater." But here, over 200 lines into the poem, we still do not know what his main subject will be, and we may be excused on first reading for thinking that the story of Ceyx and Alcione constitutes the poem's central plot.

Other breaches of narrative decorum not noted by the narrator—breaches that have led many early critics of the poem to think that Chaucer was not in control of it—add to the narrator's early admission of trouble.[10] The start of the dream phase as well as the narrator's waking period contain thwarted narratives, whole scenes that are seemingly insignificant, peripheral figures who become central, and central figures who become peripheral. The emperor Octavian seems an important figure in the dream, but he does not emerge as one. The narrator, though he joins the hunt, does not get so much as a glimpse of Octavian, and when the hounds lose the hart's scent, our narrator simply walks away. The small dog that follows the narrator at this point promises to be an unimportant figure but, instead, provides the catalyst for one of the narrative's most important transitions;[11] following the whelp, the narrator enters the "floury grene," and in this spot he finally comes upon the man in black.

Aside from these episodes that thwart expectation—a named emperor who never appears and a small, unnamed dog who leads the narrator to the Black Knight—the dream sequence of singing birds takes up a full twenty-five lines but seems to amount to nothing more than an elaborate explanation of how birdsong woke up the narrator in his dream. The narrator's description of his dream room also seems pointless to any narrative progression. The initial dream passages do indicate that the dreamer has read a great deal of French poetry as well as Latin and French versions of classical legends, but they do not lead to any kind of narrative complication, climax, or denouement. All equally important to the narrator, all joined by the conjunction "and," these early passages seem to replicate associative dream logic; they do not hint at which scenes are, or will be, crucial to the development of a story.[12]

This kind of narrative structure, following a strict chronology of events in the dream, is described by the twelfth-century theoretician Geoffrey of Vinsauf as the path of nature:

Ordo bifurcat iter: tum limite nititur artis,
Tum sequitur stratam naturae. Linea stratae
Est ibi dux, ubi res et verba sequuntur eumdem
Cursum nec sermo declinat ab ordine rerum.
Limite currit opus, si praelocet aptior ordo
Posteriora prius, vel detrahat ipsa priora
Posterius. (87–93)

[Order can take a double road: at times it advances through the by-paths of art; at times it follows the path of nature. We follow the straight path when words and events follow the same course, when the discourse does not depart from the natural order. The work runs in by-paths if a more apt order places what comes last first, or puts the first last.]¹³

Geoffrey goes on to say that an artful arrangement of material is preferable to a natural arrangement;¹⁴ he calls an artificial ordering of events, where the end or the middle of a narrative is related first, more fertile [*fertilis*] than a natural arrangement.¹⁵ But Chaucer, in the *Book of the Duchess*, seems to discount the narrative aesthetic advanced by Geoffrey of Vinsauf.¹⁶ In the poem, Chaucer's narrator follows the straight "path of nature"; the narrator's experience is related to us in the same order as it was supposed to have occurred. Still, nowhere else in Chaucer's canon is verisimilitude an end in itself, and this narrator seems to admire those who can do differently, those who can tell of their experiences or of the experiences of others according to the "by-paths of art."

Indeed, internal evidence identifies the Black Knight's tale as markedly different from that which precedes it. The Middle English word for story or narrative account, *tale*, is most often used in the *Book of the Duchess* by the narrator to name what the man in black says, though the narrator first uses it to name the romance of Ceyx and Alcione: "Amonge al this I fond a tale / That me thoughte a wonder thing. / This was the tale: There was a king / That highte Seys, and had a wif" (60–63). *Tale* usually occurs more than once in a short space, as in the lines above. At the close of the narrator's retelling the romance, he calls the romance a *tale* three times in the space of seven lines:

> For thus moche dar I saye wel:
> I had be dolven everydel
> And ded, ryght thurgh defaute of slep,
> Yif I ne had red and take kep
> Of this tale next before.
> And I wol telle yow wherefore:
> For I ne myghte, for bote ne bale,
> Slepe or I had red thys tale
> Of this dreynte Seys the king
> And of the goddes of slepyng.

> Whan I had red thys tale wel
> And overloked hyt everydel,
> Me thoghte wonder yf hit were so. (221–33)

This repetition of *tale* calls attention to the noun, as the narrator seems to say much the same thing three times over: he would still be wide awake if he had not read this tale.

Once asleep and dreaming, the narrator does not, as we might expect, call the story of Troy or the *Roman de la Rose* a *tale*, both of which he sees depicted on the windows and walls of his room. Perhaps because they are images rather than narrative accounts the narrator does not consider them *tales*. Instead, the next instance of the term denotes the narrator's first efforts to communicate with the man in black: "Anoon ryght I gan fynde a tale / To hym, to loke wher I myght ought / Have more knowynge of hys thought" (536–38). The Oxford *Chaucer Glossary* defines this use of the noun *tale* as "something to say,"[17] but the resulting modern translation ("and right away I began to find something to say to him") connotes small talk, while the narrator here seems to be embarking on a much more ambitious and goal-oriented task than simply passing the time. The narrator's purpose—to "Have more knowynge of hys thought"—suggests that he must probe this man, a stranger, who he knows is grieving the death of his lady. The only instance in the poem where the narrator identifies his own efforts as a *tale*, this passage emphasizes the extent to which the narrator must arrange and order his comments to the man in black. As we shall see, the narrator's own poem, called simply a "sweven in ryme" (1332), does not seem to demand of the narrator the same kind of ordering activity.

The narrator then succeeds in getting the knight to rehearse the origin of his sorrow—at this point couched in terms of a chess game with Fortune. When the knight ends this first monologue, the narrator calls it a *tale*: "And whan I herde hym tel thys tale / Thus pitously, as I yow telle, / Unnethe myght y lenger dwelle— / Hyt dyde myn herte so moch woo" (710–13). The knight's second long monologue is also termed a *tale*, this time by the knight himself: "But wherfore that y telle my tale?" (1034). It is interesting to note that, before beginning this second story in which he tells how he met his lady and describes her appearance, the knight demands assurance from the narrator that the narrator will pay close attention: "I telle the upon a condicioun / That thou shalt hooly, with al thy wyt, / Doo thyn entent to herkene hit" (750–52). The narrator's obtuse response to the knight's first attempt to relate the conditions of his grief prompts this demand, and he predicates the telling of an extended story (this second monologue is 282 lines long) on the condition that the audience, in this case the narrator, do its part.[18]

After this short interchange with the narrator, the knight continues to vouch for his lady's beauty, and he then describes at length the effect his lady had upon him. Like the good courtly lover that he is, the knight suffered alone in his love-longing and could not at first speak to the lady. But he finally becomes courageous enough to tell her of his sorrow. This *tale* of the knight's, referred to as such three times in the space of fourteen lines, is exceedingly short—though the narrative build-up to it is quite long—for it consists of just one word: "mercy."

> In hope of that, my tale I tolde
> With sorwe, as that I never sholde.   (1199–1200)

> For many a word I over-skipte
> In my tale, for pure fere
> Lest my wordes mysset were.
> With sorweful herte and woundes dede,
> Softe and quakynge for pure drede
> And shame, and styntynge in my tale
> For ferde, and myn hewe al pale—
> Ful ofte I wex bothe pale and red—
> Bowynge to hir, I heng the hed.   (1208–16)

Like Troilus when he first speaks to Criseyde, the knight initially falters in his lady's presence before regaining his composure to relate his full *tale*. Still, his story is ineffectual: "And whan I had my tale y-doo, / God wot, she acounted nat a stree / Of al my tale, so thoghte me" (1236–38). Unfortunately, his lady also proves not to be a good audience at first, and only after a year of service to her does the knight convince her of his worth.

Thus, Chaucer's narrator uses the word *tale* in the poem to refer primarily to the romance of Ceyx and Alcione he recites and to the extended narratives of the man in black, to those parts of the poem he presents as not his own. The Black Knight himself refers to his own monologues as *tales,* both those he directs to the narrator and those he tells his lady as he woos her. The one-word *tale,* "mercy," seems to qualify because of the knight's intent to say more and because of his efforts to organize and control his love-longing with language. The initial attempt of the narrator to communicate with the knight is labeled a *tale,* also because of the efforts made to arrange his overture artfully. But the narrator's other work, the poem we read, is simply a "sweven in ryme" (1332), and organizes itself naturally, as in Geoffrey of Vinsauf's account: "the discourse does not depart from the natural order."[19]

Separating and linking these two sections of the poem—the narrator's "natural" account of events, albeit studded with a few *tales,* and the Black Knight's "artful" love narrative—lies the garden, a version of the French *paradys d'amours* widely used as a *locus* for love tales, love debates, and similar pleasurable pastimes. Some critics have called this outdoor area a wilderness, or natural forest, because of its dense canopy of leaves.[20] Others have seen in it a place of dark, earthbound sinfulness. For example, Bernard Huppé and D. W. Robertson, Jr., claim that this grove "is a typical earthly paradise whose delights are transitory. The branches shade the grass and flowers so as to form a sort of 'via tenebrosa' whose shadows indicate oblivion."[21] This view seems to me highly problematic, however, since the conventions of the earthly paradise originated in the Mediterranean where shade was deemed a positive feature.[22] We should note that Dante's earthly paradise is also shaded "sotto l'ombra perpetua" (*Purg.* XXVIII.32) [beneath an everlasting shade].[23] Further, orchards and well-ordered groves of trees were part of extensive aristocratic and royal pleasure grounds. Piero de' Crescenzi's treatise recommended, for "the gardens of kings and other illustrious and rich lords," that "a grove of diverse trees should be planted, into which wild creatures placed in the garden may fly and hide," and elsewhere in the largest gardens "a construction with walks and bowers made entirely of leafy trees" should be made for the comfort and pleasure of the king, queen, and their "barons and lords."[24] But even the smaller gardens of one to four acres should contain a variety of fruit trees, regularly spaced.[25] Indeed, the man in black is found in such a well-groomed forest, where:

> . . . every tree stood by hymselve
> From other wel ten foot or twelve—

> So grete trees, so huge of strengthe,
> Of fourty or fifty fadme lengthe,
> Clene withoute bowgh or stikke,
> With croppes brode, and eke as thikke—
> They were nat an ynche asonder—
> That hit was shadewe overal under. (419–26)

Because of the regularity of the trees' spacing—de' Crescenzi stipulates ten or twelve feet between smaller kinds of trees, twenty feet between larger ones—Chaucer here describes part of an extensive pleasure garden, probably walled, possibly existing at some distance from the main manor house or castle. Figure 5, from a manuscript of Piero de' Crescenzi's treatise, depicts a well-tended grove. The great profusion of trees portrayed here would certainly shade the ground, would give cover to wild animals (note the birdhouses), and could provide a spot for isolated meditation such as the Black Knight's.

With its welcome shade, soft green grass, and abundance of flowers, Chaucer's garden in the *Book of the Duchess* also resembles the literary *paradys d'amours*. In fact, Chaucer draws much of his description directly from the *Roman de la Rose*, taking a few lines from several different places in the poem. As noted by editors of the poem, the lines of Flora and Zephirus are derived from the *Roman* (8411–30), as is the image of the earth vying with the heavens (*Roman* 8430ff.). Chaucer's passage on how the spot has forgotten the "povertee" it suffered during winter is also based on the *Roman* (53–66), as are both the detailed description of how the trees are spaced and clipped (1370ff.) and the catalogue of animals Chaucer's narrator sees (1375ff.). Finally, Chaucer appears to have taken the figure of Argus, the great calculator, from much later in the *Roman* (12,790–96).[26]

Viewed in this way, Chaucer's garden description consists of a patchwork of lines loosely translated from the *Roman*, but in all cases, Chaucer's narrator has succeeded in highlighting both his knowledge of the *topos* and, unwittingly, his status as a foreigner, of one not entirely comfortable with the French idiom.[27] That Chaucer could have translated the passages more precisely can be assumed by comparing the Middle English translation of the *Roman* attributed to Chaucer with the French original.[28] Guillaume de Lorris describes the woods he entered in his dream thus:

> Li bois recuevrent lor verdure,
> Qui sont sec tant come ivers dure;

Convention and the Poet in Two Early Dream-Poems   45

Figure 5. Wooded park, Piero de' Crescenzi, *Livre des proffits ruraux*, book VIII, ca. 1470, Bruges. New York, Pierpont Morgan Library, MS. M.232, fol. 205 v.

> La terre meïsmes s'orgueille
> Por la rosee qui la mueille,
> E oblie la poverté
> Ou ele a tot l'iver esté.   (53–58)

The Middle English translation follows the French closely, in rhyme scheme and metrical stress as well as in syntax:

> These wodes eek recoveren grene,
> That drie in wynter ben to sene,
> And the erthe wexith proud withalle,
> For swote dewes that on it falle,
> And the pore estat forget
> In which that wynter had it set.   (57–62)

In the *Book of the Duchess*, however, Chaucer has broken the passage's self-contained nature by rhyming it with the preceding and succeeding lines: the six lines follow the pattern a bb cc d, instead of the original aa bb cc. Further, Chaucer's version changes the order of the images: Guillaume de Lorris begins with the recovery of spring and then contrasts it with the poverty of winter, thus following Geoffrey of Vinsauf's artful arrangement of narrative material. But Chaucer starts with winter's sorrow, which is then followed by nature's regeneration during spring, thus following a natural progression of events:

> Hyt had forgete the povertee
> That wynter, thorgh hys colde morwes,
> Had mad hyt suffre, and his sorwes;
> All was forgeten, and that was sene,
> For al the woode was waxen grene;
> Swetnesse of dew had mad hyt waxe.   (410–15)

The result of Chaucer's changes is an awkwardness not found in the original French or in the Middle English translation. The line that concludes the image of regeneration—"Swetnesse of dew had mad hyt waxe"—is a seemingly unnecessary explanation of the process, a clumsily added afterthought whose rhyme straddles two sections of the garden description. The corresponding explanation in the French original occurs in the middle of the six-line passage, as it does in the Middle English translation, where it seems integral to the passage.

Similarly, Chaucer's narrator explains who Flora and Zephirus are: "They two that make floures growe" (403). While a much longer explanation accompanies the mention of them in Jean de Meun's lines (8403ff.),

Chaucer's version again highlights the explanation as intrusive. Both poets separate the subject—Flora and Zephirus—from the verb—*had; estendaient*—but the grammatical awkwardness seems inconsequential in the French version; there the reader is expected to dwell instead on the masterful description that culminates in the poetic conceit of the flowers vying with the stars in their brilliance and number:

> Zephirus e Flora sa fame,
> Qui des fleurs est deesse e dame,
> (Cist dui font les floretes naistre;
> Fleurs ne quenoissent autre maistre,
> Car par tout le monde semant
> Les va cil e cele ensement,
> E les fourment e les couleurent
> Des couleurs don les fleurs eneurent
> Puceles e vallez preisiez
> De beaus chapelez renveisiez,
> Pour l'amour des fins amoureus;
> Car mout ont en grant amour eus)
> De floretes leur estendaient
> Les coutes pointes, qui rendaient
> Tel resplendeur par ces erbages,
> Par ces prez e par ces ramages,
> Qu'il vous fust avis que la terre
> Vousist emprendre estrif ou guerre
> Au ciel d'estre meauz estelee
> Tant iert pour ses fleurs revelee. (8411–30)

[Zephirus and his wife Flora, the goddess and lady of flowers, spread out for men the counterpanes of little flowers. (These two make flowers spring up. Flowers know no other master, for he and she go together throughout the whole world sowing flowers; they shape them and color them with those colors that the flowers use to bring honor, in gay and beautiful chaplets, to young girls and men who, with the love of pure lovers, value each other because of their great love.) The little flowers that they spread out reflected such splendor among the grass, the meadows, and the woods that you would have thought that the earth was grown so haughty on account of its flowers that it wanted to take up war with heaven over the question of which had the better field of stars.][29]

Chaucer's explanatory line, in contrast, is direct and matter-of-fact, but far more obtrusive:

> For both Flora and Zephirus,
> They two that make floures growe,
> Had mad her dwellyng ther, I trowe.   (402–4)

In short, while producing a description of a place that is clearly the *locus amoenus* turned love park of his French source, Chaucer also draws attention to the fact that his narrator is either new to the conventional *topos* or for some other reason not as conversant in it as the poets he seeks to emulate.

That Chaucer's audience was familiar with such descriptions of gardens is clear from the narrator's insistence that they need not ask whether there were many green branches: "Hyt ys no nede eke for to axe / Wher there were many grene greves, / Or thikke of trees, so ful of leves" (416–18). The lines presume an audience keen on such descriptions, eager for a full account, as well as a narrator fully aware that he is playing to his audience's expectations. Trying to emulate the French poets with whom his audience is so well acquainted, this narrator fails to do so seamlessly—he draws attention to the process of emulation and evinces Chaucer's parody of the French idiom, of the English desire to emulate the French, and of an audience that hungers for recognizable descriptions of conventional continental *topoi* like the garden.

The rise of English nationalism during the Hundred Years' War with France has been well documented. Still, as Donald Howard and Janet Coleman have pointed out, no English literary tradition could be called on to replace the French tradition so important to the English aristocracy and to court literature.[30] A wholesale rejection of French conventions, *topoi*, and idioms was impossible for an English poet of the period since such a rejection would have left the English poet without a storehouse of conventions upon which to draw—in effect, without a poetic language. Chaucer's treatment of the garden *topos* here both acknowledges his necessary dependence on the *topos*, as it was known to his audience through

French versions, and articulates his critical distance from it. Chaucer's narrator wants to write a description of a garden that will please an audience that dotes on the *Roman de la Rose*; Chaucer wants to depict the limitations of his narrator's desire and to expose it to the scrutiny of the same audience that expects its poet to emulate French models.

Chaucer also achieves critical distance with humor in the passage. Chaucer's narrator exaggerates conventional elements and he renders idealized elements of the *topos* commonplace. The superabundance of animals in the *paradys d'amours* prefigures the crowded field of birds in the *Parliament*. Here, the narrator claims that "Argus, the noble countour" would "fayle to rekene even / The wondres me mette in my sweven" (435–42). These wonders include:

> And many an hert and many an hynde
> Was both before me and behynde.
> Of founes, sowres, bukkes, does
> Was ful the woode, and many roes,
> And many sqwirelles that sete
> Ful high upon the trees and ete,
> And in hir maner made festes.   (427–33)

Unlike his counterpart in the *Roman* (1375ff.), only a spectator, Chaucer's narrator occupies the same space as these animals, who are both behind him and in front of him. Further, Chaucer's squirrels not only play on the boughs overhead, they "made festes," and we can almost hear them cracking acorns.

An ambivalent attitude toward French precursors is also evident in the poem as a whole. The Black Knight's tale, while more coherent and satisfying as a narrative, is nevertheless full of French literary idioms that Chaucer's narrator does not understand and that have struck many readers of the poem as overused and outmoded.[31] The narrator's account, however, while less satisfying as a plotted narrative, nevertheless provides us with an original portrait of an individual, appealing to many critics who call it particularly "Chaucerian."[32] In Geoffrey of Vinsauf's terms, Chaucer's narrator prefers the "by-ways of art" but, left to his own devices, is capable only of pursuing the straight path of nature. Chaucer, on the other hand, seems to prefer the path of nature, or at least to have important reasons for using it in this poem.

The chronological ordering of events is itself, of course, an artistic device, an artificial way of arranging material that gives the impression that it follows the sequence of events as they actually occurred. All narratives, naive and complex alike, are the result of artistic choices, of leaving out some events or aspects of events in favor of others. The question then arises: why has Chaucer in the *Book of the Duchess* chosen to represent what his narrator claims is the way events actually happened in the order in which they happened? Again, Geoffrey of Vinsauf advises:

> Si quis habet fundare domum, non currit ad actum
> Impetuosa manus: intrinseca linea cordis
> Praemetitur opus, seriemque sub ordine certo
> Interior praescribit homo, totamque figurat
> Ante manus cordis quam corporis; et status ejus
> Est prius archetypus quam sensilis. Ipsa poesis
> Spectet in hoc speculo quae lex sit danda poetis.
> Non manus ad calamum praeceps, non lingua sit ardens
> Ad verbum: neutram manibus committe regendam
> Fortunae; sed mens discreta praeambula facti,
> Ut melius fortunet opus, suspendat earum
> Officium, tractetque diu de themate secum.
> Circinus interior mentis praecircinet omne
> Materiae spatium.   (43–56)

[If anyone is to lay the foundation of a house, his impetuous hand does not leap into action: the inner design of the heart measures out the work beforehand, the inner man determines the stages ahead of time in a certain order; and the hand of the heart, rather than the bodily hand, forms the whole in advance, so that the work exists first as a mental model rather than as a tangible thing. In this mirror let poetry itself see what law must be given to poets. Let not your hand be too swift to grasp the pen, nor your tongue too eager to utter the word. Allow neither to be ruled by the hands of fortune but, in order that the work have better fortune, let a discrete mind, walking before the deed, suspend the offices of both hand and tongue, and ponder the theme for a while. Let the inner compasses of the mind lay out the entire range of the material.][33]

Geoffrey advises the writer to ponder his material first. But at the close of the *Book of the Duchess,* Chaucer's narrator awakes, finds the book of Ceyx and Alcione still in his hands, and says that he determined then and there to put his dream into rhyme: "Thoghte I, 'Thys ys so queynt a sweven / That I wol, be processe of tyme, / Fonde to put this sweven in ryme / As I kan best, and that anoon'. / This was my sweven; now hit ys doon" (1330–34). This narrator does not first decide how best to arrange the material, or that "the inner compasses of the mind [will] lay out the entire range of the material." The overt aesthetic is to record the dream quickly, as best he can, letting the natural order of events in the dream organize the poem. The phrase "be processe of tyme" signifies that the dream will be rehearsed in time, that is, chronologically, and does not seem to carry with it the sense of measured and careful consideration that a modern rendering of the phrase might suggest, since Chaucer's narrator will commit his dream to paper "anoon."[34]

Chaucer's interest in this aesthetic is, I believe, twofold. Fascinated with the way narratives are formulated, Chaucer presents much seemingly preliminary, nonnarrative material. He does not give us a thesis statement, an overarching thematic framework, as Geoffrey of Vinsauf advises, but he has us discover the man in black and his story by trial and error just as the narrator himself does. Second, Chaucer is concerned to depict the sacrifices inherent in the creative process, in the process of choice that necessarily eliminates many potential elements of a narrative in order to bring others into focus. As critics have noted, the progress of this poem resembles the process of writing a poem.[35] As the writer of dream-poems needs dreams in order to write, it is possible to read the narrator's initial insomnia as a kind of literary barrenness, or writer's block. He cannot sleep, therefore he cannot dream, and therefore he cannot write. His insomnia, though, leads him finally to read, and his reading leads him finally to sleep. Implicitly, then, reading for this narrator is a means to writing. Not only do his consequent dream and poem take elements from the romance he has read, but the act of reading leads to the act of writing, via the dream.

But once the narrator is asleep and dreaming, it takes some time before he arrives at the "real subject" of the poem—the tale told by the man in black. As noted above, he goes through several experiences that seem unrelated and distinctly nonnarrative. These passages have independent, lyriclike integrity and follow each other without being causally connected to one another: the chorus of birds, the literal depiction of the *Roman de la Rose* and the story of Troy, and the hart-hunt. These separable passages refer clearly to conventional genres: the heavenly sound of the birds to passages in the *Roman* and several French *dits,* the depiction of the *Roman* to an entire corpus of interconnected literature to which the *Roman* gave rise, the story of Troy to several redactions of that story, and the hunt to several sources and analogues in English and continental romances and the Breton *lais* of Marie de France.[36] Chaucer refers here not only to seminal works but to the works spawned by them—to the whole process of texts begetting more texts. Indeed, in the early dream phase, it seems the narrator is looking for, even trying out, various kinds of narratives. Lisa Kiser has noted that Chaucer's "natural and his literary heritage is appropriately evoked as part of a bedroom milieu because it is within that room of dreams that he works so diligently at 'making'."[37] I would add that the narrator's literary heritage is not just "evoked" but is actively tried out in the poem.[38] This poem articulates a journey of discovery for its narrator. De Certeau's assertion that walking through the landscape is an act of *"appropriation* of the topographical system" pertains to Chaucer's dream-poems; movement through space in these poems creates meaning, delineates choices, and stakes out personal claims. In the *Book of the Duchess,* Chaucer's narrator seems to be searching for a literary genealogy—a family of narratives into which he may insert one of his own, and he seems to try out, albeit briefly, several generic forms.

It is only when the narrator enters the *paradys d'amours* and discovers the man in black that the narrative begins to progress in a way we recognize as productive of storytelling. Even though the story told by the knight is not itself altogether coherent—he tells his story in more than one way, and he has a difficult time getting the narrator to understand him—still, we are treated to a story: that of the knight's winning of his fair lady White, and his subsequent loss of her. The effect is that of a narrator stumbling into the material for a poem and showing us, step by step, exactly what he went through to achieve the narrative, including the trial of several narrative types or genres that, in this poem, do not overtly relate to the central story, though, as many critics have written, they do relate in various covert ways. Barbara Nolan has called this narrator a *"bricoleur*—finding his materials as if by chance, piecing them together in astonishing new ways," which seems to me an apt characterization. She continues by defining this narrator as a "nonparticipa[nt] in established conventions . . . freed from the demands of familiar mythologies by his refusal to embrace expected authoritative stances in relation to his audience, matter, and meaning."[39] But it seems to me that Chaucer's narrator in the *Book of the Duchess* realizes that he *must* adhere to the "demands of familiar mythologies" in order to be understood; he must situate his own narrative in a generic context, in a family of interrelated narratives, using whatever tools of the trade convention can provide for him.

Other critics have also viewed convention as a negative force against which Chaucer's narrator must strive. Dieter Mehl has written that "The real importance of *The Book of the Duchess* . . . [lies] in the distinctly personal and suggestive appeal the poet has succeeded in creating out of an unpromisingly conventional literary form."[40] R. A. Shoaf has similarly invoked "a poetry which transcends the conventions of amorous rhetoric as it strives to recover the reality of Love."[41] But conventional literary form *is* the language a poet inherits, and just as communication in English or some other language is possible only by grammatical convention, communication in literary texts is possible only by literary convention. Instead of viewing the narrator as one who is imprisoned by conventions from which he must free himself, convention itself is the poet's language. As Kathryn Lynch has demonstrated in her study of the philosophical dream vision, "adherence to convention can supply a kind of meaning too."[42] Indeed, the *Book of the Duchess* celebrates the wealth of conventions available to this well-read poet, as Chaucer adapts and revises conventional *topoi*.

Chaucer's choice of the *paradys d'amours*, a continental *topos* that had been used extensively by French court poets, seems to signal the direction his story will take. The garden introduces the reader to a familiar place—the *locus* of love debates, love complaints, lovers' meetings—and prepares us for the genre of a lover's tale that follows. In addition, the description of the *paradys d'amours*, based on conventional language, serves with the preceding lyriclike passages as the narrator's apprenticeship in miniature, as well as the threshold to a longer and more conventional narrative. Chaucer's narrator finds that he must choose one story over several others and stick to it. He must write within a narrative tradition (for example, the *Roman de la Rose*, the story of Troy, or the romance) because narratives beget other narratives and are not generated *ex nihilo*, and because poems cannot be written or understood in a cultural or generic vacuum. Finally, the fact that the nature of Chaucer's narrative changes once the poet has entered the well-ordered space of the garden points to the importance of the garden, and of convention in general, to Chaucer's conception of narrative organization. The fact that Chaucer chooses to show us this transformation rather than have it happen in the "inner compasses of the mind," out of our view, also signals his desire to have his audience focus on the process of constructing a narrative from found materials, and his desire to illustrate what is left out when he enters into the conventional *tale* of the man in black. Other critics have located the *Book of the Duchess* within a context of coming of age for Chaucer as a poet.[43] I submit that whether or not it was Chaucer's first lengthy narrative poem, it details a concern that was central to all his poetry and that surfaced in many different ways: his knowledge and use of poetic convention and his singularly ambivalent relationship with conventional language.

With the *Parliament of Fowls,* probably written within a decade after the *Book of the Duchess,* Chaucer addresses these same issues of narrative structure and poetic genealogy. Several thwarted narratives, separable lyriclike passages, and internal evidence that this narrator too has difficulty getting to the point of his story all contribute to making the first three hundred lines of the *Parliament* another exercise in inconclusive narrative. In addition, the narrative pattern—Introduction, Reading, Sleep, Dream, Entrance into the garden, and Event(s)—is repeated in the *Parliament* with one particularly significant variation. Once the narrator enters the walled park, he encounters two models for the experience of love: the Temple of Venus and the parliament of birds. While the narrator's encounter in the *Book of the Duchess* with the man in black leads to a single tale, albeit a tale told as a result of dialogue with the narrator, in the *Parliament* the narrator encounters a multiplicity of voices and varying points of view, to which he is a spectator rather than a full participant in the dialogue.

But initially, like his counterpart in the *Book of the Duchess,* this narrator acknowledges that he has difficulty getting to his "first mater." Three times he draws attention to the fact that his narrative rambles. At line 17, after the opening meditation on the cruelty of the god of Love as presented in books, the narrator asks: "But wherfore that I speke al this?" Just nine lines later, the narrator again corrects himself: "But now to purpos as of this matere" (26), which leads to his version of the dream of Scipio. At line 113, the narrator invokes Cytherea and appears to be starting the poem anew just as he begins to tell his dream, a correspondence that underscores the similarities between a dream and a poem discussed above. And finally, at line 372, after his description of the garden and the Temple of Venus, the narrator begins a new stanza with: "But to the poynt: Nature held on hire hond / A formel egle" (372–73). Only after this do we overhear, with the narrator, the proceedings of the parliament of birds, the event that many readers consider the "heart" of this poem and that lends its name to the poem as a whole by Chaucer's admission in his Retraction to the *Canterbury Tales.*

Thus the opening 371 lines of this poem are considered by the narrator preliminary and not "to the poynt"; critics as well have often privileged the parliament in their discussions, finding this final section a kind of resolution, even though the inner plot of the "formel" eagle is not resolved at all.[44] Yet, as in the *Book of the Duchess,* a few hundred opening lines are difficult to discount, even though the narrator would have us do so. Indeed, they articulate many of the issues a writer of narratives must resolve before he writes a conventionally successful narrative.

H. Marshall Leicester, Jr., has argued persuasively for the "unifying project" of the narrator of the *Parliament,* whose sense of unity is under severe pressure from an increasingly fragmented society. The narrator proceeds with difficulty for two reasons: "first, the multiplicity, richness and variety of the authoritative traditions, conventions, literary models, lore, etc., that Chaucer is aware of in his culture; and second, his own subjectivity—the multiplicity, richness and variety of his particular interests and perceptions."[45] Conflict also resides in the lengthy description of the walled park, as well as in other parts of this poem, and the garden serves as an appropriately discordant threshold between the narrator's confusion about how to write a love poem and his extreme discomfort at the Temple of Venus, and then again between the Temple of Venus and the unresolved debate of the parliament.[46] As with other received conventions, the garden evinces the "multiplicity, richness and variety of the authoritative traditions" with which Chaucer grapples in the *Parliament.*

The narrator's first impression of the wall that encloses the park—that it is green—may refer to its being covered with moss, to its age. A walled garden itself recalls both the biblical *hortus conclusus* and the walled *paradys d'amours* of the *Roman de la Rose,* both models Chaucer knew and drew on extensively. In contrast, the sign over the entrance, painted in black and gold, seems new, or at least not obscured by the passage of time. In the juxtaposition of the overgrown wall that recalls, in part, the *Roman*'s painted wall and the clearly legible sign that recalls the entrance to Dante's *Inferno* there may be an allusion to the changes wrought by Dante on the by-then conventional love park of the *Roman de la Rose*.[47] While this notion of the historicity of the two *topoi* is reversed, as Dante's version of the earthly paradise is of an older lineage than Guillaume de Lorris's description of the walled love park, from Chaucer's point of view it may be that Dante's *Commedia* was seen as an effort to subsume erotic, courtly love, portrayed in the *Roman* and other poems, into the overall scheme of the Christian pilgrimage toward the celestial paradise. But whatever the relationship between the *Roman* and the *Commedia* implied here, Chaucer's narrator's relationship to them both is marked by ambiguity. Like the wall in the Song of Songs, this wall seems to veil and protect an inner realm still unknown to the narrator. But unlike the wall of the *Roman* on which many allegorical figures are depicted, this wall stands mute, obscured by moss, or simply not painted. The sign over the gate, while legible and written in plain English, nevertheless presents contradictory statements and so gives the narrator no clear information about what he may find within the park. This radical ambiguity does not diminish once the narrator has entered the park but is sustained by the description of the idealized landscape, which consists of a series of stanzas derived from different garden *topoi*.

Once inside, the narrator's first impression of the inner realm recalls descriptions of the earthly paradise—a place of perpetual spring, untouched by time—as well as Boccaccio's description of Cytherea's temple in the *Teseida:* "For overal where that I myne eyen caste / Were treës clad with leves that ay shal laste, / Ech in his kynde, of colour fresh and greene / As emeraude, that joye was to seene" (172–75).[48] Like Cytherea's temple in Boccaccio's poem, this spot is shaded by trees, but where Boccaccio names pine trees, Chaucer implies deciduous trees that never drop their leaves, thus emphasizing the connection with the timelessness of the earthly paradise. The narrator's joy at entering the garden recalls Dante's description of his entrance into the earthly paradise, although the perfect spot is achieved with far less effort by Chaucer's narrator and his guide than by Dante's.[49] Further, Chaucer's introduction of emeralds as a simile describing the green color of the leaves owes more to gemstones found in French descriptions of love parks, as well as to the descriptions of the new Jerusalem in Revelation 21:18–21, than they do to anything in Boccaccio's setting. And so, with this simile, Chaucer may signal that his earthly paradise is also a paradise of love, drawing both from the biblical passage as well as from the French *dits*.

But the next stanza contains a catalogue of trees, a *topos* found in a later section of the *Teseida* (11.22–24) and in a host of other texts known to Chaucer:

> The byldere ok, and ek the hardy asshe;
> The piler elm, the cofre unto carayne;
> The boxtre pipere, holm to whippes lashe;
> The saylynge fyr; the cipresse, deth to playne;
> The shetere ew; the asp for shaftes pleyne;
> The olyve of pes, and eke the dronke vyne;
> The victor palm, the laurer to devyne.   (176–82)

While there is precedent for a catalogue of fruit trees in a love park, most notably in the *Roman* (1347–56), this particular list, with the trees identified by their usefulness, is primarily an epic convention, recalling the gathering of wood for a hero's funeral pyre. Its inappropriateness to any description of the perfect spot would have been evident, I think, to Chaucer's audience. In fact, its primary function here, as a "bravura interlude" in Curtius's phrase, seems to be to draw attention to itself and to the narrator's poetic virtuosity.[50] But the passage also stands out because it is alien to a description of the perfect spot, be it an earthly paradise or a paradise of love. Chaucer's narrator here wants to show off his poetic sophistication; Chaucer shows us with this stanza the narrator's poetic ineptitude.

The narrator's unabashed mixing of *topoi* relating to nature continues in the third stanza of the garden description as he returns to the *paradys d'amours* of his French predecessors and Boccaccio's Temple of Venus:

> A gardyn saw I ful of blosmy bowes
> Upon a ryver, in a grene mede,
> There as swetnesse everemore inow is,
> With floures white, blewe, yelwe, and rede,
> And colde welle-stremes, nothyng dede,
> That swymmen ful of smale fishes lighte,
> With fynnes rede and skales sylver bryghte.   (183–89)

A resemblance to the gardens of his French predecessors is inescapable. The beautiful meadows and variety of fruits and flowers recall Machaut's and Froissart's love gardens.[51] But when Chaucer's narrator adds that he saw "nothyng dede" in the stream, we are again made aware of this narrator's unsophisticated poetic sensibility. We do not expect any dead leaves or fish to float in an idealized stream. In addition, the assertion emphasizes the narrator's presence in the scene as he seems to be drawing a comparison between his present perception of an idealized garden and his past experience of actual streams.

The fourth stanza of description is closer to Boccaccio's Temple of Venus passage than any of the others, and I reproduce them both below:

> On every bow the bryddes herde I synge,
> With voys of aungel in here armonye;
> Some besyede hem here bryddes forth to brynge;
> The litel conyes to here pley gonne hye;
> And ferther al aboute I gan aspye
> The dredful ro, the buk, the hert and hynde,
> Squyrels, and bestes smale of gentil kynde.   (190–96)

> Quivi sentì pe' rami dolcemente
> quasi d'ogni maniera uccei cantare,
> e sovra quelli ancor similemente
> li vide con diletto i nidi fare;
> poscia fra l'erbe fresche prestamente
> vide conigli in qua e 'n là andare,
> e timidetti cervi e cavriuoli
> e altri molti varii bestiuoli.   (VII.52)

The comparison of birdsong to the harmony of angels Chaucer has imported from the *Roman,* again to underscore the association with the earthly paradise.[52] But the abundance of birds is to be found in Boccaccio's stanza, and the lists of animals in the two passages are quite similar. A few small changes are not in my opinion significant: Chaucer's substitution of the bringing forth of baby birds for the building of nests and his omission of any mention of new grass on which Boccaccio's rabbits play seem not to alter the passage's conventional meaning. The English version, however, contains an ambiguity the Italian does not in its translation of *timidetti* as *dredful*. Boccaccio's *cervi* are themselves timid. Chaucer's *ro* can be seen as either timid, full of dread, or as frightening to one looking on, terrifying. Both meanings are attested in English by 1250. Further, at the start of the *Parliament*, the narrator speaks of a "dredful joye"—terrifying happiness—an oxymoronic and conventional phrase in love poetry that establishes the possibility of a double entendre here.

Similarly, the penultimate stanza describing the idealized spot seems at first to be based firmly in literary models detailing the harmonious sounds and light breezes of the earthly paradise or *locus amoenus*, including Boccaccio's passage in the *Teseida*, also quoted here:

> Of instruments of strenges in acord
> Herde I so pleye a ravyshyng swetnesse,
> That God, that makere is of al and lord,
> Ne herde nevere beter, as I gesse.
> Therwith a wynd, unnethe it myghte be lesse,
> Made in the leves grene a noyse softe
> Acordaunt to the foules song alofte.   (197–203)

> Similemente quivi ogni strumento
> le parve udire e dilettoso canto;
> onde passando con passo non lento
> e rimirando, in sé sospesa alquanto,
> dell'alto loco e del bello ornamento,
> ripieno il vide quasi in ogni canto
> di spiritei, che qua e là volando
> gieno a lor posta; a' quali essa guardando,
>
> tra gli albuscelli, ad una fonte allato,
> vide Cupido fabricar saette,
> avendo alli suoi piè l'arco posato,
> le quai sua figlia Voluttà selette
> nell'onde temperava.   (VII.53–54)

Again, one adjective stands out: *ravyshyng*. Not a soothing sweetness of sound, this sound ravishes, seizes, abducts the listener. It may, of course, be translated as "enchanting,"[53] but it seems to me that it must carry with it at least an undertone of violence. This, with the possible ambiguity of "dredful ro" of the preceding stanza, combines to color the generally positive tenor of the description. While it may be overstating the effect to speak of the appearance of a terrifying deer and a sound that seizes the listener violently, the seemingly perfect scene contains imperfections—the possibility for violence and terror that is an element alien to most of the garden *topoi* Chaucer inherited. The narrator's earlier comment about the absence of dead fish may also unexpectedly raise the specter of death. Of course, we may here recognize the *hortus deliciarum* of Jean de Meun's poem, the Garden of Déduit, which "makes the living drunk with death."[54] And the ambiguous nature of this space—is it paradise or is it hell?—lends the poem some of its unsettled quality.

But further, this sort of ambiguity in the passage depends entirely on the reader's interpretation of the words in context and, as such, points to another concern of this narrator: the extent to which the entire scene depends only on his perception of it in his dream and his description of it in the poem. Throughout, Chaucer's narrator follows Boccaccio's emphasis on what the narrator sees and hears: "saw I," "I gan aspye," and "herde I" translate Boccaccio's repetition of "vide" and "senti" throughout the description in the *Teseida*. But Chaucer goes further with his emphasis on personal perception noted above as early in the passage as line 175: "that joye was to seene." This is not an absolute state of joy the narrator describes, but a joy produced in the narrator by his looking at the green leaves. What Boccaccio conveys with the qualifying phrases "le parve udire" (stanza 53) and "le sembiava" (stanza 51), Chaucer conveys with a variety of phrases that call into question the absolute nature of the perfect spot.[55]

Traditionally, one of the identifying characteristics of the perfect spot is that it exists eternally, outside the acts of men and women, in a realm that does not change and does not depend on human perception of it. In Dante's *Purgatorio*, for example, his entrance into the earthly paradise is a transcendent experience. He is accommodated to the timelessness of the place. Dante's lines on the earthly paradise do not emphasize his own perception but describe the ways in which the changeless place impressed itself on him: "Un'aura dolce, sanza mutamento / avere in sé, mi feria per la fronte / non di piú colpo che soave vento" (*Purg.* XXVIII 7–9) ["My forehead felt the stirring of sweet air, / whose flowing rhythm always stayed the same, / and struck no harder than the gentlest breeze"].[56] With Chaucer, perhaps characteristically, the opposite effect rules: the timeless nature of the perfect spot is modulated by the narrator's perception that the spot exists only in his description of it. It exists as it seems to him to exist, not absolutely whether or not he is there to describe it. In Chaucer's poetry, language takes on, quite literally, creative and constitutive power, with all the problems of interpretation and phenomenology that that implies. If the garden of paradise exists primarily in poetic descriptions of it, then does it truly exist? And if we know something like the perfect spot only through human representations of it, then how perfect can it really be?

The final stanza of Chaucer's description, before the narrator sees Cupid and all of Cytherea's attendants, articulates the dilemma of the poet describing the earthly paradise, or any other idealized spot:

> Th'air of that place so attempre was
> That nevere was grevaunce of hot ne cold.
> There wex ek every holsom spice and gras;
> No man may there waxe sek ne old;
> Yit was there joye more a thousandfold
> Than man can telle; ne nevere wolde it nyghte,
> But ay cler day to any mannes syghte.   (204–10)

Timeless and absolute, this place holds people in suspension as well: "No man may there waxe sek ne old." In addition, this spot defies description by humans: there is more joy there "Than man can telle." But at the same time, it can only be known by humans through language and perception: it is never night there but always a clear day "to any mannes syghte." Thus, human language is both inadequate for describing paradise and necessary for its description. Further, the last line begs the question: does the spot appear differently to the sight of angels? To God? To those animals "of gentil kynde" alluded to in line 196? That the spot may appear differently to different creatures makes it seem nonabsolute, dependent entirely on the perceptions of the narrator rather than on any quality that is inherently and eternally present.

What is noteworthy in this long sequence of stanzas is the way in which the conventions for garden and park descriptions jostle one another. Specifically, the classical *locus amoenus* is not walled, a catalogue of trees and their usefulness is an epic convention and not part of the descriptions of a *locus amoenus* or of the earthly paradise, and references to timelessness do not have a place in descriptions of French love parks or gardens. In short, these *topoi* do not mesh, despite the insistence in the passage on an overall sense of unity and well-being. An audience educated in these *topoi* would realize immediately the discordant nature of the passage—the intrusion of one set of conventional elements into another set, of one model breaking into another. While it is true that these *topoi* are themselves subject to change, as in the case of the garden of love emerging as a medieval application of the *locus amoenus*, Chaucer's version mixes previously unmixed elements and would have seemed jarring to his contemporaries. As Robert Worth Frank, Jr., points out: "A literary convention can be convincing only so long as there is no intrusion of an element not accepted by the convention."[57] This covert jostling of authoritative discourse prefigures the mix of attitudes about love and love poetry the narrator next encounters in the Temple of Venus and the realm of Nature. In both places of love, housed within the mixed paradise of love, the narrator continues to receive conflicting information and to respond in a subjective manner, highlighting the fact that it is his dream. The "mater of to wryte" (168) that the narrator had been promised at the poem's start by Affricanus turns out to be a treasure trove of traditional images and genres from which he must choose. That the description of the garden shares many elements with the description of the heavenly realm in Macrobius's *Somnium scipionis* is, of course, no accident but suggests that the "mater of to wryte" is a paradise for this narrator. As one who actively seeks a poem, Chaucer's narrator in the *Parliament* brings Chaucer's treatment of his own poetic self-consciousness to the foreground. As one who is overwhelmed by the choices available to him, Chaucer's narrator also raises issues of literary creation and narrative.

In both the *Book of the Duchess* and the *Parliament of Fowls*, then, we witness the process by which the narrator's undirected experiences (his insomnia, reading, and dream) lead to a coherent tale (the tale told by the Black Knight; the Temple of Venus and the parliament of birds) and are given shape and meaning by the tale that follows. It is not surprising that much criticism of the poems focuses on how parts of the early narrative relate to the later sections, as they appear to be much better thought-out and artful in Geoffrey of Vinsauf's sense than the earlier passages. The man in black does follow Geoffrey's advice—his narrative begins with the statement that his lady is dead, and this knowledge frames and organizes his tale. Similarly, both the narrator's experience of the Temple of Venus and the parliament of birds are organized by authority figures, Venus and the goddess Natura. But Chaucer steadfastly refuses to organize his dream narratives in any similar way. When his narrator enters the garden, he enters a world that is organized according to Geoffrey of Vinsauf's principles. Typically, Chaucer's narrator is *in* but not *of* that world. David Lawton has argued that in the *Parliament* "Nature stands for the kind of order we impose and have to impose on the external world, in order to perceive and in order to think."[58] I would add that Chaucer's explicit ordering activity extends to the Temple of Venus as well as to the Black Knight—everything, in sum, that occurs within gardens in these two early poems.

One might expect these gardens to serve as points of transition and transformation for the narrators who enter them. In many of Guillaume de Machaut's poems, for example, narrators and characters who enter love parks and gardens emerge from them with new understanding, a new outlook.[59] But in Chaucer's early dream-poems, it is the narrative itself that changes—the storytelling activity—and not the narrator. Chaucer creates opportunities for critiquing, parodying, and questioning convention with his narrators' obtuseness, even blindness. A nonlover in a love garden and a nonpoet in a garden of literary plenty, Chaucer's narrators articulate the distance between Chaucer and received convention, a distance that also informs Chaucer's use of conventional garden *topoi* in the *Troilus*.

— 3 —

Troilus and Criseyde:
A *Paradys d'Amours* Lost

In his early dream-poems, Chaucer addresses directly issues of a poet's dependence on earlier poems, and he shows us the selective, creative process at work. With *Troilus and Criseyde,* probably completed by 1386, Chaucer engages once again in the practice of *translatio* and again uses a narrator who is acutely self-conscious about the process of constructing a new text out of earlier ones. From his opening lines that briefly trace the conventional story of Troilus to the closing stanzas of book V in which our narrator instructs his "litel book" (V.1789) to "subgit be to alle poesye" (V.1790), this narrator consistently acknowledges his debt to his predecessors and to preexistent poetic models.[1]

Further, Chaucer juxtaposes in *Troilus and Criseyde* a set of ideal values, principally those associated with what has come to be called "courtly love," with a perceived reality or set of circumstances that prevent the full realization of those ideal values.[2] Other critics have differed on the significance of the juxtaposition, with Charles Muscatine maintaining that the ideal of courtly love is outdated by Chaucer's time, Barry Windeatt centering his analysis on the "divergence between the experience and the description of love," and Karla Taylor writing that Chaucer critiques the language used to describe both the ideal of love and ideal Christian truths.[3] But a look at Chaucer's use of gardens in the poem reveals an aspect to the critique of courtly love not noted by previous scholars. In the juxtaposition of ideal love with seemingly real situations and social pressures, Chaucer's poem demonstrates the weakness of ideal values when confronted with a society inimical to those values—we witness the fragility of a value system not upheld or reinforced by social convention. Gardens become a visual analogue for the ideal love affair promulgated in medieval romances, satirized by Andreas Capellanus, and commemorated in innumerable lyrics. But the gardens' protective walls weaken metaphorically under the weight of social convention so that the garden, which appears to offer a safe haven to the lovers and their secret affair, in fact offers no protection, only an illusion of safety. So too the code of courtly love, with its convention of secrecy, turns out not to shield Troilus and Criseyde from the forces that eventually separate them physically from one another, but to contribute to a situation that they cannot control.

Chaucer's changes to Boccaccio's *Il Filostrato*, his base text in reworking the story of Troilus, have been well documented by several critics, most of whom have extended or reformulated the notion first articulated by C. S. Lewis that Chaucer "medievalized" Boccaccio's poem. Robert Payne identifies six "principal areas of [rhetorical] elaboration"; David Wallace meticulously details "Chaucer's reactions to the language, syntax and prosody of the Italian poem"; and Windeatt's work focuses on Chaucer's use of romance conventions, especially in his reworking of Boccaccio's main characters.[4] But Chaucer also wrought changes in the poem's setting, in the public and private spaces of the Italian poem, both defining Boccaccio's spaces more fully and adding—"in-eching"—several of his own creation.[5] The pattern of Boccaccio's thematic use of space in the love affair survives in Chaucer's poem. Chaucer's Troilus, like Boccaccio's Troilo, originally spots Criseyde at a public temple, and the parting scene in both poems occurs on an open plain between Troy and the Greek camp. Chaucer thus reproduces the two public spaces, the temple and the plain, that frame the private love affair. But Chaucer transforms many of the private spaces of his poem, particularly those where the two lovers contemplate an affair before their first private meeting. Often, where Boccaccio uses a private room, Chaucer uses a garden, which is at once less private than Boccaccio's rooms and more clearly informed by a courtly love aesthetic and ideal. Further, in Boccaccio's version, the only garden of the poem occurs at the zenith of the love affair, while Chaucer not only keeps that garden at the end of book III, but adds four others that precede it.

These changes in setting draw attention to the context of courtly love that C. S. Lewis and others argue Chaucer added to the Italian Renaissance poem, as these "in-eched" gardens draw on French poems and the *topos* of the *paradys d'amours*, contributing to a pattern of associations that Chaucer added to his source in order to highlight the conventional nature of courtly love. Further, gardens provide the setting for three of the poem's lyrics on love—one supposedly sung by Troilus and overheard by Pandarus, a second one sung by Criseyde's niece Antigone, and a third by Troilus at the end of book III.[6] Not only do these lyrics underscore the role of the garden as a spot for thinking and singing about love, but they too help in establishing an ideal of love as the perfect union of two individuals—as a blessed state to be intensely desired.

Both courtly love, with its conventions and rules, and the pleasure garden, with its requisite features, establish guidelines for appropriate behavior. Both attempt to regulate those who would submit to such control. Entering a pleasure garden, one is encouraged by its landscape to walk in a leisurely fashion, to linger beside the fountain, to sit for a time on its turf bench. Entering an affair governed by the rules of courtly conduct, one is encouraged to steal glances, to steal moments together, to steal one's private pleasure from the rush of public life, to keep one's affair a secret. The narrator of *Troilus and Criseyde* acknowledges the conventional nature of courting when he writes:

> For every wight which that to Rome went
> Halt nat o path, or alwey o manere;
> Ek in som lond were al the game shent,
> If that they ferde in love as men don here,
> As thus, in opyn doyng or in chere,
> In visityng in forme, or seyde hire sawes;
> Forthi men seyn, "Ecch contree hath his lawes."   (II.36–42)

In each country different rules apply, and such rules are not to be neglected for, if one ignores them, the "game" of love is "shent." In Chaucer's poem, the *paradys d'amours* with its connotations helps summon up the context of courtly love, not only by its association with French *dits amoureux*, but also by its highly charged nature in the world in which Chaucer lived.

But first, a brief look at Boccaccio's use of setting is in order. Boccaccio's lovers become acquainted in public spaces, move into private rooms both to deliberate the act of falling in love and to meet as lovers, and the two return to the public arena when they part during the exchange of prisoners. At the happiest point of their affair, near the end of canto III, Troilo leads Pandaro to a garden and there exclaims his poem to Venus:

> O luce etterna, il cui lieto splendore
> fa bello il terzo ciel, dal qual ne piove
> piacer, vaghezza, pietate ed amore,
> del sole amica, e figliuola di Giove,
> benigna donna d'ogni gentil core,
> . . .
> prolunga, cela, correggi e governa
> il mio ardore e quel di questa a cui
> son dato, e fa ch'io non sia mai d'altrui.   (III.74, 89)

[O light eternal, whose untroubled radiance makes beautiful the third heaven, whence are poured down pleasure, desire, pity, and love, friend of the sun and daughter of Jove, gracious mistress of every gentle heart. . . . Prolong, keep secret, correct, and govern my ardour and that of her to whom I have given myself, and grant that she shall never be another's.][7]

The light apostrophized in this passage shines especially strongly in contrast with the scenes that precede and succeed it. The first time Troilo and Criseida meet they do so in darkness, in a "secret place" with just one torch lighting the way.[8] After Troilo's paean to Venus, he is suddenly plunged into darkness in canto IV when news of the exchange of Creseida for Antenor drives him not only into his room, but also causes him to have the windows shuttered against daylight:

> E verso il suo palagio se ne gio,
> sanza ascoltare o volgersi ad alcuno,
> e tal qual era sospiroso e pio,
> sanza voler compagnia di nessuno,
> nella camera ginne; e che disio
> di riposarsi avea, disse; onde ognuno,
> amico e servitor, quantunque caro,
> n'uscì, ma pria le finestre serraro.
> . . .
> Rimaso adunque Troiolo soletto
> nella camera sua serrata e scura.   (IV.22, 26)

[And he made his way towards his palace, without listening and turning to anybody, and sighing and cast down as he was, wishing the company of nobody, went into his room and said he wished to rest. And thus everybody, friends and servants, however dear, went out, but first they closed the windows ... Troilus was thus left alone in his closed and dark chamber.]⁹

The only garden in Boccaccio's poem, not itself described, accompanies the full flowering of the love affair. Its association with light—both with the natural light of day and with the metaphorical light apostrophized in the lyric—contrasts with the two scenes of darkness that surround it and underscores its significance in the poem.

Chaucer's use of gardens and other spaces in the *Troilus* is at once more straightforward than that I have outlined for *Il Filostrato* and more complex. On the one hand, each garden immediately announces itself as a setting for courtly activities by means of a specialized vocabulary and a set of conventional garden features, including such items as a fountain and turf benches. On the other hand, this clear signification of each garden does not neatly fit a pattern of love and of loss, whereby the lovers *might* enjoy their love in such beautiful settings before being cast, like Boccaccio's Troilo, into literal darkness and despair or out of the garden. Rather, these conventional gardens and their corresponding lyric interpolations help in establishing a "horizon of expectations" for the affair, an ideal against which the actual affair is then measured and judged.[10] But the actual love affair must respond to pressures not acknowledged by the ideal, the pressures of a social context that determines many of the lovers' actions. Troilus's apparent unwillingness to marry Criseyde, or Criseyde's unwillingness to marry Troilus, and their inability to deny her father's claims on her all contribute to the outcome of the poem. Still, these social and political forces do not at first impinge on the love affair, which is repeatedly conceived of and spoken about in beautiful garden settings.

Pandarus, the great schemer, in effect creates the first garden of the poem when he tells Criseyde about the lovesick Troilus. Claiming that one day, not long ago, he and Troilus were in the palace garden (which may be his or Priam's[11]), Pandarus creates a scene that, as far as we know, never happened:[12] "This other day, naught gon ful longe while, / In-with the paleis gardyn, by a welle, / Gan he and I wel half a day to dwelle" (II.507–9). Pandarus says that they spoke of an ordinance, of military strategy, and that they played at throwing spears. Then, he continues, Troilus lay down to sleep on the grass:

> Tyl at the laste he seyde he wolde slepe,
> And on the gres adoun he leyde hym tho;
> And I afer gan romen to and fro,
> Til that I herde, as that I welk alone,
> How he bigan ful wofully to grone.   (II.514–18)

Troilus's groan turns into a well-composed complaint to the God of Love, recited—and possibly created—by Pandarus for Criseyde's benefit. Like the gardens in the *Roman de la Rose*, Jean Froissart's *Le Paradys d'Amours*, and other poems, this palace garden is enclosed, and it contains a well and a grassy spot for reclining. Like lovers who inhabit these gardens, Troilus lies down in order to sleep, but he appears to desire only the privacy that sleep affords and instead speaks to the God of Love: "He seyde, 'Lord, have routhe upon my peyne, / Al have I ben rebell in myn entente; / Now, *mea culpa*, lord, I me repente!'" (II.523–25). The *paradys d'amours*, also identified as the court of the God of Love in some continental poems, including Boccaccio's *Filocolo*, provides the perfect spot for talking, thinking, dreaming, and singing about love.

In addition, Troilus's lyric articulates conventional attitudes about love's joy and pain. Charles Muscatine calls Troilus "*too* perfect a courtly lover," claiming that "In him convention has taken on the superior purity that is only possible in nostalgic retrospection." Windeatt adds that Troilus's "identification with the life of romance heroes has been emphasized by Chaucer's adaptation of his immediate source."[13] Most notably, Pandarus has Troilus present Criseyde as the enemy in love. And when Troilus asks the God of Love to be his shield against "disesperance" (II.530), immediately followed by his reference to the wounds Criseyde has inflicted on him, the God of Love appears as the protector for Troilus against the assaults of Criseyde's beauty: "For certes, lord, so soore hath she me wounded, / That stood in blak, with lokyng of hire eyen, / That to myn hertes botme it is ysounded, / Thorugh which I woot that I moot nedes deyen" (II.533–36). Indeed, if Pandarus has made up the lyric, he has marshaled the entire tradition of lovers who fall asleep on grassy meads and banks as a way of legitimating Troilus's love for Criseyde. And if he simply reports Troilus's words here, as he claims, Troilus himself has successfully internalized the tradition. Without knowledge of the original scene, we cannot gauge the integrity of Pandarus's version. We know only that once Troilus sees Criseyde in the temple he rides home and closes himself into his bedroom to bemoan his fate; Pandarus comes upon Troilus in his room. So when Pandarus relates the scene of Troilus making a complaint in a garden, he may very well have fabricated it in order to impress upon Criseyde the hard fact of Troilus's love-pain.[14] Further, whether the original lyric took place in Troilus's room or in a garden, Pandarus *uses* the garden image effectively here, packaging and marketing Troilus in a way that he hopes might impress Criseyde. And, since Criseyde is given to reading with her ladies as a way of passing the time (II.82ff.), Pandarus wisely assumes she knows what such a garden context might mean: namely, that Troilus is a conventional courtly lover; that his life will be miserable until and unless Criseyde rewards him with her "mercy," a euphemism for female surrender to male desire; and that Crisedye will be called on to play the role of the beloved, whether she likes it or not.

Initially, Criseyde does not seem to like it at all. Surprised and disappointed that her uncle advises her to love Troilus, when he should forbid it (II.413),[15] Criseyde worries about her loss of "estat"—the loss of her stature in a community that has already been shaken by her father's treason—and control over her own possessions, which, as a widow, she could easily lose to her male relatives.[16] It is not surprising that Criseyde cannot immediately see the advantages for herself in such an arrangement, and she initially refuses to participate in the game of courtly love Pandarus is intent on setting in motion.

The second garden of the poem belongs to Criseyde's palace. Once Pandarus has told her of Troilus's love (and of the love-song overheard in the garden), Criseyde thinks about Troilus and about the dangers of falling in love again. Troilus then happens to ride by her house beneath the window of her private closet. This chance sighting has the effect of strong drink or of a love potion on Criseyde, prompting the much-quoted line "Who yaf me drynke?" (II.651). After additional reflection, she leaves her closet in a heightened emotional state and goes down the stairs into her garden, where her three nieces and a "gret route" (II.818) of other women accompany her. The narrator describes her garden, particularly its architectural details: "This yerd was large, and rayled alle th'aleyes, / And shadewed wel with blosmy bowes grene, / And benched newe, and sonded alle the weyes, / In which she walketh arm in arm bitwene" (II.820–23). Like Troilus's garden, as evoked by Pandarus, Criseyde's garden resembles a literary *paradys d'amours*, with its turf benches and gravel paths. With the mention of welcome shade, its debt to the classical *locus amoenus* is also clear. But here, an emphasis on the architecture, on those elements in the garden that have been constructed from wood, sand, and brick, along with an emphasis on the excellent condition of the garden, distinguishes Criseyde's garden as a physical space that seeks to emulate a literary space. While Pandarus evokes Troilus's garden in highly charged, conventional language, the narrator describes Criseyde's garden in very concrete, physical terms, impressed by the new turf benches, by railings along each pathway, and by the fresh sand in those paths. I believe we can distinguish here between a self-consciously literary *topos*—Troilus's garden as described by Pandarus—and what we are supposed to feel is a physical, actual garden—Criseyde's. Playing a literary *topos* against a description of a seemingly physical space is one of Chaucer's mimetic tricks. The heightened literariness of one garden makes the other seem real, and vice versa. Still, both gardens are self-consciously created spaces, and both allude to the conventional rules and games of courtly love.

Indeed, Antigone sings a song about love's pleasures in Criseyde's garden in which she gives voice to part of the courtly ideal latent in the garden itself—love is perfect bliss, which is not surprising given its probable source in several of Guillaume de Machaut's poems, including *Le Paradis d'Amour* and *Mireoir amoureux*:[17] "Ye, blisful god, han me so wel byset / In love, iwys, that al that bereth lif / Ymagynen ne kouthe how to be bet" (II.834–36). This view of love contrasts with Criseyde's reservations about entering an affair with Troilus—in her words "Unhappes fallen thikke / Alday for love" (II.456–57). Nevertheless, the image of perfect bliss presented in Antigone's song causes Criseyde to entertain second and third thoughts about an affair with Troilus, and this scene, while not arranged by Pandarus, serves his purposes well.[18] Similar to the first time Troilus rides by Criseyde's window, also not arranged by Pandarus, this panegyric to love helps entice Criseyde to enter that "game" about which she expresses so many reservations.

But on closer inspection, Antigone's lengthy paean to love contains contradictory information concerning actual love experience. The song, after introducing love as bliss, berates those who rail against love's rule, saying that nothing good comes about without sorrow: "No wele is worth, that may no sorwe dryen" (II.866). Thus the song admits—however fleetingly—that love does in fact bring sorrow. While presenting a seemingly straightforward portrait of love without pain ("ther is no peril inne" [II.875]), it also asserts by implication that sorrow is an unavoidable corollary to love's joy.[19] Like Troilus's lyric recited by Pandarus, Antigone's song adheres closely to the codes of courtly love; it evinces a central paradox of the love experience as both joyful and sorrowful. However, Antigone's song does not present the paradox in a series of conventional oxymorons, as Troilus does early in book I:

> If no love is, O God, what fele I so?
> And if love is, what thing and which is he?
> If love be good, from whennes cometh my woo?
> If it be wikke, a wonder thynketh me,
> When every torment and adversite
> That cometh of hym may to me savory thinke,
> For ay thurst I, the more that ich it drynke.   (I.400–406)

Antigone's dual perspective lacks the conventional equation of love's joy with sorrow, but speaks instead of an experience that includes both joy and sorrow, and therefore strikes a more realistic note than do Troilus's love songs. Just as Criseyde's garden seems real compared to Troilus's, so too Antigone's song seems closer to a description of an actual experience when compared both with Troilus's song in book I and with Pandarus's creation (or record) of Troilus's complaint in book II. The seemingly real love experience seeks to emulate the ideal at the same time as it helps to point up the conventional, artificial nature of the ideal.

Indeed, Criseyde responds to Antigone's song as the record of individual experience rather than as conventional wisdom. She inquires after the song's author, and Antigone's answer, that "the goodlieste mayde / Of gret estat in al the town of Troye" (II.880–81) wrote the song, seems to satisfy Criseyde that love may not jeopardize her "estat" after all.[20] Criseyde sighs as she contemplates the validity of the song's claims, and the garden setting again seems to do its cultural work: Criseyde wants to believe in love's purported bliss, and she wants to believe that her reality can match the idealism of the courtly code. The narrator's emphasis on the created reality of Criseyde's garden and Criseyde's emphasis on the experiential aspect of Antigone's song suggest that Chaucer meant to paint Criseyde as a realist to Troilus's portrait as an idealist, as many have argued. In addition, the purported reality of the garden and the lyric serves to remind us of the highly artificial nature of the literary *paradys d'amours* and of the unalloyed bliss of erotic love as described in lyric song, just as

Criseyde's relatively realistic concerns about love serve as a foil to Troilus's hopelessly idealistic vision. Still, both Criseyde's realism and Troilus's idealism lead them to an affair. Criseyde's garden and Antigone's song work their magic as surely—and perhaps more convincingly for Criseyde—as Troilus's garden and lyric did before them.

Criseyde's garden also provides the setting for her receipt of Troilus's first letter via Pandarus. Pandarus says he seeks the privacy a garden can offer: "Into the gardyn go we, and ye shal here / Al pryvely, of this a long sermoun" (II.1114–15). Even though other members of the household are present in the garden, Pandarus carefully sits beyond their hearing: "And whan that he so fer was that the sown / Of that he spak no man heren myghte, / He seyde hire thus, and out the lettre plighte" (II.1118–20). Not only a stage for love songs, then, the manor garden also promises a measure of privacy—aural privacy within a medieval household and visual privacy from one's neighbors. A walled city garden was desirable then as it is now, and for many of the same reasons: as a refuge from the press of urban life, as a way of claiming part of the natural world for one's own private pleasure, and as a very physical representation of the exclusion of outsiders from an elite, upper-class household. The narrator of the *Troilus* refers indirectly to the pleasure garden as an image of protection from the outside world, when, early in book III, he claims Criseyde felt Troilus to be a steel wall or shield for her: "That wel she felte he was to hire a wal / Of stiel, and sheld from every displesaunce" (III.479–80). According to the narrator, "displesaunce" remains outside their relationship; by extension, "plesaunce," another word for a pleasure garden, is what the two enjoy, albeit on a metaphorical dimension only, since Troilus and Criseyde never meet in an outdoor *plesaunce*. Despite Chaucer's creation of several pleasure gardens for this version of the story, he does not include one for Troilus and Criseyde. In this, they are distinguished from another pair of lovers, or potential lovers, Helen and Deiphebus.

The poem's third garden, attached to Deiphebus's house, provides the setting for Deiphebus and Helen to spend an entire hour alone, supposedly reading a letter from Hector, as a result of Pandarus's machinations to get Troilus and Criseyde together in Deiphebus's bedroom:

Deiphebus gan this lettre for t'onfolde
In ernest greet; so did Eleyne the queene;
And romyng outward, faste it gonne byholde,

> Downward a steire, into an herber greene.
> This ilke thing they redden hem bitwene,
> And largely, the mountance of an houre,
> Thei gonne on it to reden and to poure.   (II.1702–8)

Deiphebus and Helen must descend from the bedroom to the garden, probably by means of an outdoor staircase, and they reenter the bedroom by the same stairs 250 lines later: "With that Eleyne and also Deiphebus / Tho comen upward, right at the steires ende; / . . . / She [Criseyde] took hire leve at hem ful thriftily," (III.204–5, 211). It seems likely that Pandarus knew Helen and Diephebus would welcome the privacy of the "herber greene" and occupy themselves there while Pandarus worked to fulfill his plan for Troilus and Criseyde's first meeting. After all, Helen married Deiphebus after Paris's death.[21] Indeed, this scene further ties gardens to love-talk and courtly dalliance, and while we are not privy to Helen and Deiphebus's conversation in his garden, their stolen hour serves as a backdrop to the first semiprivate meeting between Troilus and Criseyde, and the narrator himself joins in lyric praise of love with the proem to book III. Opening with a series of apostrophes, as does Boccaccio's hymn to Venus, Chaucer's narrator's version nevertheless includes one appositive phrase, "Plesance of love," (III.4) of his own invention. Again, Chaucer invokes the *plesaunce*, the love garden, Troilus and Criseyde never visit together, as if such a place exists for them only metaphorically. The privacy they require does not allow them outdoors together, where a member of their household could see them. Helen and Deiphebus do not feel such constraints, which suggests how differently their relationship is represented in the poem.

Other changes Chaucer made in Boccaccio's hymn to Venus color the rhetoric of universal equilibrium and harmony a distinctly courtly hue, including a reference to "gentil hertes" (III.5) and the identification of the narrator as Venus's clerk (III.41). In particular, Chaucer changes dramatically a stanza on the influence Venus has over Mars. Boccaccio's stanza mentions several negative traits that Venus banishes from an individual suffering from love, including anger and vileness:

> Tu 'l fiero Marte al tuo piacer benegno
> ed umil rendi, e cacci ciascuna ira;
> tu discacci viltà e d'alto sdegno

> riempi chi per te, dea, sospira;
> tu d'alta signoria merito e degno
> fai ciaschedun, secondo ch'el disira;
> tu fai cortese ognuno e costumato
> che del tuo foco alquanto è infiammato.   (III.77)

> [Fierce Mars, thou dost render benign and humble to thy will, and thou dost drive out all wrath. Thou dost banish vileness and dost fill him who sighs for thee, O goddess, with lofty pride. Thou dost make each deserving of and fit for high power according to his desires. Thou makest each one who is at all kindled with thy flame courteous and of good bearing.]²²

Chaucer, in contrast, emphasizes the last lines of Boccaccio's version by inserting mention of courtly behavior throughout the stanza:

> Ye fierse Mars apaisen of his ire,
> And as yow list, ye maken hertes digne;
> Algates hem that ye wol sette a-fyre,
> They dreden shame, and vices they resygne;
> Ye do hem corteys be, fresshe and benigne;
> And heighe or lowe, after a wight entendeth,
> The joies that he hath, youre myght it sendeth.   (III.22–28)

The mention of "hertes digne" in the second line; the image of being set ablaze in the third line; the allusion to dreading shame, being courteous, "fresshe," and kind in the next two lines; and finally the mention of both higher and lower joys, where Boccaccio only refers to "alta signoria," marks Chaucer's version with the knowledge of those sensual pleasures Venus controls as well as the ennobling influence that she exerts on her followers.

In the following stanza as well Chaucer changes the tenor of Boccaccio's lines, alluding more pointedly to the mysteries of sexual attraction. Boccaccio refers in a general way to harmonious union between individuals:

> tu sola le nascose qualitadi
> delle cose conosci, onde il costrutto

vi metti tal, che fai maravigliare
chi tua potenza non sa ragguardare.   (III.78)

[Thou alone knowest the hidden qualities of things, by which thou dost contrive such harmony as to cause wonder in him who knows not how to see thy power aright.][23]

But Chaucer refers directly to the attraction between a man and a woman:

Ye knowe al thilke covered qualitee
Of thynges, which that folk on wondre so,
Whan they kan nought construe how it may jo
She loveth hym, or whi he loveth here,
As whi this fissh, and naught that, comth to were.   (III.31–35)

The crucial question for Chaucer's narrator is not philosophical, celestial, or abstract, but is firmly fixed in the human experience of love. While this narrator may begin with the general "thilke covered qualitee / Of thynges," he descends or reverts to the specific "whi this fissh" with characteristic alacrity. To the extent that this lyric interlude can be said to take place in a garden, it joins Pandarus's recital of Troilus's lyric and Antigone's paean to love in establishing a "horizon of expectations" for the affair that depends on the courtly code of conduct.

Still, the crucial scene at the start of book III, the scene on which our attention is focused, does not occur in the garden but in a bedroom. This substitution of the bedroom for the garden suggests a series of contrasts between the two couples—Helen and Diephebus, Criseyde and Troilus—rather than similarities.[24] One couple apparently can risk being seen by members of the household, as the two take the air about the garden, but the other couple appears unable or unwilling to risk similar exposure. The importance of secrecy to Troilus and Criseyde reinforces the highly conventional way in which they seem to conceive of their love for one another.[25] To avoid the appearance of impropriety, Criseyde must hurry out of the bedroom at Deiphebus's house when she hears Helen and Deiphebus's footsteps on the stairs. Indeed, one of Andreas Capellanus's maxims about courtly love, "Amor raro consuevit durare vulgatus" ["Love does not usually survive being noised abroad"],[26] informs their behavior throughout the tale.

The poem's last garden scene, late in book III, and the only one in the Italian version, follows the consummation of the love affair and the establishment of regular secret meetings between Troilus and Criseyde. During this blissful period, Troilus often leads Pandarus into a garden (though whose garden it is we do not know) where he speaks of Criseyde, of "hire womanhede" (III.1740) and "hire beaute" (III.1741). On one occasion, Troilus also invokes a Boethian view of love as universal equilibrium, virtue, and heavenly accord, echoing the narrator's proem to book III. Chaucer's source for Troilus's canticum, Boethius's *Consolation of Philosophy*, book II, metrum 8, emphasizes the way love holds contraries together; drives the sun, moon, and stars; and causes the sea to remain within its boundaries. This last image of constraint, as translated by Chaucer, reads:

> And yif this love slakede the bridelis, alle thynges that now loven hem togidres wolden make batayle contynuely, and stryven to fordo the fassoun of this world, the which they now leden in accordable feith by fayre moevynges.[27]

Chaucer has Troilus elaborate the image of the bridle:

> And if that Love aught lete his bridel go,
> Al that now loveth asondre sholde lepe,
> And lost were al that Love halt now to-hepe.
>
> So wolde God, that auctour is of kynde,
> That with his bond Love of his vertu liste
> To cerclen hertes alle and faste bynde,
> That from his bond no wight the wey out wiste;
> And hertes colde, hem wolde I that he twiste
> To make hem love, and that hem liste ay rewe
> On hertes sore, and kepe hem that ben trewe!   (III.1762–71)

The activities of binding fast and encircling hearts expand on Boethius's image of the bridle of love. They also allude to the shield of secrecy that is supposed to protect Troilus and Criseyde's affair from outside disturbances. Most significantly, however, Troilus's expansion of Boethius's lyric *replaces* Boethius's lines on the bonds that hold two people together in marriage:

This love halt togidres peples joyned with an holy boond, and knytteth sacrement of mariages of chaste loves; and love endith lawes to trewe felawes. O weleful were mankynde, yif thilke love that governeth hevene governede yowr corages.[28]

For Troilus and Criseyde, the bonds of love, not reinforced by the "sacrement of mariages," contrast with Boethius's vision, and this discrepancy informs the breakdown of the love affair. Despite the increased emphasis on binding and encircling, Troilus omits mention of the one bond that could have kept the lovers together.

Not long after this song, with the opening of book IV, we enter the beginning of the end of the love affair. Criseyde is traded to the Greeks at her father's request, finally led away "by the bridel" by Diomedes (V.92), and the protection offered by Troilus's discretion, by their extensive secrecy, disintegrates. There is no legal bond to keep Criseyde in Troy; she is not married to a Trojan but is still considered the legal property of her father. Simultaneously, the *paradys d'amours* disappears from the poem, and the outer world—the city of Troy and its war with Greece—takes over. Even though the affair in private has become much more than a game for Troilus and Criseyde, the fact that they continue to follow one of the game's main precepts—secrecy—makes their relationship vulnerable to a host of outside influences. Indeed, this poem suggests that secrecy does not necessarily enhance a love affair, as Andreas Capellanus claims. Obstructions to the lovers' union may be fruitful for narrative suspense and may initially fan the flames of love, but these same obstructions in *Troilus and Criseyde* overwhelm the secret love affair, resulting in a powerful critique of the influence of literary ideals on human behavior. Again, I think we are meant to distinguish between a literary convention and an imagined reality that tries but fails to measure up to the literary ideal. The garden walls, which are supposed to keep out prying eyes and the press of urban life, have no effect when most needed. The construction of an elaborate space for the elite activity of "daliaunce" is swiftly destroyed by outsiders, by the political and other social forces it was built to exclude. Marriage seems to have no place in the garden *plesaunce,* but it is the bond of family and the social structure of the patriarchy that impinge on the bliss and harmony promised in the poem's lyric passages.

Gardens in the *Troilus* thus unambiguously provide the characters with settings appropriate to love-songs and to love-talk. Pandarus in particular seems hyperconscious of the uses such gardens can be put to, of their meaning in the culture of courtly love. Antigone, less self-consciously, reinforces the associations between manor gardens and love's purported bliss; the narrator also adds his voice when Helen and Deiphebus pair off in Deiphebus's garden while Troilus and Criseyde meet in Deiphebus's bedroom; and finally Troilus joins in with his praise of love in a garden late in book III. But the ideal, as voiced by these characters and as implied by the presence of these garden settings, cannot fully adapt itself to less-than-ideal situations and contexts. In part, the difficulties in applying love conventions to the narrative of a love affair may derive from the fact that the predominantly lyric ideal of courtly love does not function well in narrative. Joan M. Ferrante has explored the discrepancy between the function of courtly love in lyric and in early Arthurian romances which "attempt . . . to adapt the inspirational force of courtly love to the service of society."[29] Ferrante finds that in late romances "The more central the love story is to a romance, the more difficult it becomes for the author to find a comic solution to his story," and "Courtly love, which is meant to be a force for good in society, instead destroys society."[30] Indeed, narrative examples of Ferrante's conclusions include *Roman de Thèbes, Roman de Troie*, the romances of Chrétien de Troyes, the Tristan story, and Malory's *Morte Darthur*.[31] Many of Marie de France's *lais* provide an alternate outcome. That is, secret love often endures its most significant test when exposed to public view. Some of Marie's lovers successfully rejoin society, as in "Guigemar" and "Milun," while others find that their love is stronger than the bonds of social obligation, as when Lanval and his otherworldly lover leave Arthur's court for Avalun, or when Yonec's parents are reunited in death. But in Chaucer's romance, none of these outcomes is reproduced; love and society vie for the upper hand in *Troilus and Criseyde*, as they do in continental romances, but society destroys love in Chaucer's version, or at least it obstructs the love affair. Maintaining the secrecy of the affair does not guarantee its longevity, but instead contributes to its end. What is not told, the information not shared, allows Criseyde to be exchanged to the Greeks as though she were simply Calkas's daughter, without important ties to Troy.

Perhaps tellingly, Chaucer hints at an alternate ending in the lovers' last private meeting, one that would parallel the story of Piramus and

Thisbe. Informed of the unwelcome news of Criseyde's exchange to the Greeks, Troilus and Criseyde meet secretly, embrace, weep, and finally, after beseeching Troilus for help, Criseyde faints:

> "O Jove, I deye, and mercy I beseche!
> Help, Troilus!" And therewithal hire face
> Upon his brest she leyde and loste speche—
> Hire woful spirit from his propre place,
> Right with the word, alwey o poynt to pace.
> And thus she lith with hewes pale and grene,
> That whilom fressh and fairest was to sene." (IV.1149–55)

Troilus believes her dead—she is unconscious for a full eight stanzas. He prepares her body for burial and draws his sword:

> He gan hire lymes dresse in swich manere
> As men don hem that shal ben layd on beere.
>
> And after this, with sterne and cruel herte,
> His swerd anon out of his shethe he twighte
> Hymself to slen, how sore that hym smerte. (IV.1182–86)

To Troilus, suicide seems the only action appropriate to Criseyde's untimely death-by-grief. Consider for a moment how different Criseyde's reputation would be had she died, like Thisbe, rather than face separation from Troilus. This alternate ending in fact answers audience expectations of romance plot. Dido falling on her sword in the *Roman d'Aneas* and Yonec's mother dying of grief on her husband's tomb in Marie de France's "Yonec" both satisfy genre expectations in a way Criseyde's ongoing life does not.[32] Indeed, just as the garden scenes in *Troilus and Criseyde* help identify the discrepancy between convention and an imagined reality, so too Criseyde's clearly articulated departure from the model romance heroine points up the discrepancy between conventional romance plot and the reality Criseyde and Troilus must face.

The examination of convention in this poem echoes to some degree that of the early dream-poems. There, the juxtaposition of conventional, plotted narrative with a rambling, plotless narrative points up the sacrifices inherent in tale-telling. Some of what the poet must leave out of his tale appears as the plotless preamble, the surplus of experience, which must be severely truncated in the service of tale-telling conventions Chaucer inherited from the continent. Similarly, in *Troilus and Criseyde*, Chaucer juxtaposes the highly developed conventions of courtly love with a world of social and political circumstances that exist separately from the system. The inability of the courtly system to respond to these outside forces resembles the failure of conventional narrative patterns to represent or incorporate seemingly extraneous material. The relationship between the ideal of courtly love and the actual love affair is represented in the discrepancy between the protected precinct of the ideal pleasure garden and its complete failure to protect the lovers whose affair depends so completely on the ideal. The language of courtly convention in *Troilus and Criseyde* establishes a "horizon of expectations" that, once established, allows Chaucer to expose its limits and shortcomings. Chaucer portrays both a well-defined system and a world that does not mesh with that system. What results from this meeting is, in the narrator's words, "myn tragedye" (V.1786), despite Troilus's transcendent vision of his earthly experience.

To what extent, then, does Chaucer condemn the use of convention in *Troilus and Criseyde*? Does he acknowledge its necessity at the same time that he exposes its shortcomings? As argued above, Chaucer represents clearly the power of conventional systems over individual behavior in the poem. One additional example should suffice. As Criseyde debates inwardly the possibilities of a love affair with Troilus in book II, she vacillates between two roles: the calculating widow and the conventional courtly object of male desire. At one extreme, Criseyde coolly analyzes her own social position in Troy and her desire for autonomy (or, rather, for her perceived autonomy), and she acknowledges her fear of being the subject of male desire and control: ". . . Allas! Syn I am free, / Sholde I now love, and put in jupartie / My sikerness, and thrallen libertee?" [II.771–73]. At the other extreme, she envisions Troilus the perfect knight, perfectly worthy of her love: "And [she] gan to caste and rollen up and down / Withinne hire thought his excellent prowesse, / And his estat, and also his renown, / His wit, his shap, and ek his gentilesse" [II.659–62]. Troilus's chivalric appearance, his "prowesse" as he comes from battle, his high "estat" in Troy, and his apparent "gentilesse" all appeal to Criseyde's notions of the ideal knight and potential lover.[33]

Indeed, without the language and the trappings of courtly love, without the context of the *paradys d'amours* and the imperative of secrecy, how would the two have spoken to one another in the first place? What language, what discourse of love would remain for them had Chaucer chosen *not* to use the paradigm he did? The Ovidian legacy of erotic sexuality, of female artistry and male quest, which Boccaccio draws on in *Il Filostrato*, might have served, but it would have generated a different kind of poem, one much closer in spirit to Boccaccio's.[34] Other discourse models for the expression of romantic love are scarce. To feel that particular kind of erotically charged and ennobling love is to have already submitted to the courtly paradigm. Courtly love creates Western romantic love as we currently conceive of it, and Chaucer had no other mold from which he could create such a love for Criseyde and Troilus. But as in his dream-poems, Chaucer does not submit to convention without drawing attention to his submission, and without articulating all that is lost by the act of submission. This is not to say that I believe Chaucer thought men and women could communicate without recourse to conventional narrative modes. I do not posit an ideal state that would discard convention for some sort of "natural," nonrhetorical, nongeneric, nontraditional language. Language, as is true of all forms of communication, depends on convention, on genre, on a set of predetermined signs that have cultural significance. And while authors may play with these signs—parody them, subvert them—they cannot give them over entirely without also giving up the whole enterprise of communication.

— 4 —

Gendered Paradises in *The Canterbury Tales*

In the Wife of Bath's description of Jankyn's book of wicked wives, a certain Latumyus tells his friend: "That in his gardyn growed swich a tree / On which he seyde how that his wyves thre / Hanged hemself for herte dispitus" (III.759–60). To which his friend replies: "Yif me a plante of thilke blissed tree, / And in my gardyn planted shal it bee" (III.763–764). The garden as a *locus* of male domination, reinforced by the role of gardens in tales both preceding and following the Wife's, is here displayed at its most gruesome, albeit humorous in context: as the *locus* of suicide for three wives. Walled gardens and parks enclose and contain several women in the *Tales*, and come to represent in context the conventional roles that prescribe the activities of medieval women, particularly as wives or as prospective wives. As Priscilla Martin puts it: "Chaucer sees what is lovely in the garden and what is wrong with it."[1] While several tales use gardens or manicured groves, including the Squire and the Shipman, I shall concentrate in this chapter on three—the Knight's, the Merchant's, and the Franklin's—ones in which gardens figure prominently as *loci* for action involving the tales' heroines. Indeed, the three women characters discussed here—Emelye, May, and Dorigen—all inhabit fictional worlds created by male storytellers, but they nevertheless express desires and aspirations that confront or undermine male-centered conventions. Further, many of these confrontations occur in gardens or in language that derives from garden *topoi*, so gardens function in these tales both as *loci* expressing conventional expectations and as contested ground.

In the case of Latumyus's garden, the symbol of his wives' servitude to him provides them with the instrument of their deaths—a tree on which to hang themselves, and this tableau emphasizes an extreme example of male domination. Not surprisingly, in the rest of the Wife of Bath's prologue and tale, antigardens rule: open fields and forests replace enclosed gardens and signify the Wife's aversion to conventional gender roles. Gardens in the *Tales* also provide Chaucer the opportunity to show female characters transgressing conventional gender roles and, if only temporarily, escaping the confines of their duties as wives and daughters. Most notably, May of the *Merchant's Tale* discovers a way of transforming January's pleasure park into one of her own, but even the otherwise passive Emelye envisions a future other than marriage for herself in terms directly opposed to the enclosed garden that she so prettily occupies. As in the dream-poems and *Troilus and Criseyde*, gardens in the *Tales* represent the rules and regularity of convention. But while gardens in the dream-poems serve in Chaucer's meditation on literary convention and gardens in the *Troilus* serve in his critique of courtly convention, gardens in the *Tales* contribute to an examination of the social conventions surrounding marriage, specifically the roles women are called upon to perform as wives and as marriageable daughters.

Historical studies of the last fifteen years describe the status of medieval wives in a sociopolitical context. Eileen Power, summarizing her research, writes:

> We find that under English common law the unmarried woman or widow—the *femme sole*—was, as far as all private, as distinct from public, rights and duties are concerned, on a par with men. ... On the other hand when she married, her rights, for the duration of the marriage, slipped out of her hands.[2]

These rights and duties included landowning, performing homage for land, suing other parties and being sued, entering into contracts, making wills, and the like. More recently, historians have emphasized the limit to women's public power in the late medieval period while confirming, on the whole, Eileen Power's conclusions. Jo Ann McNamara and Suzanne Wemple have found that a woman's power was usually connected to her family's sphere of influence. As the power of families diminished through the eleventh and twelfth centuries, to be replaced by that of kings and great lords, the power of individual woman also declined.[3] More specific to fourteenth-century England, Judith M. Bennett's work on women's access to public power in one manor in Northamptonshire between 1287 and 1348 reveals that "women's power waxed, waned, and waxed again over the course of the female life cycle"[4] as they changed status from unmarried maiden to wife to widow. Bennett maintains that most women never attained the same or equivalent public stature to men in late medieval communities, whether married or not, but that female participation in nondomestic spheres of life did diminish markedly during marriage.

In addition, the work of Georges Duby has clarified the extent to which medieval women were unable to choose how they lived their own lives. Husbands were often chosen for girls at a very early age by the girl's father or legal guardian; girls could be betrothed during their childhood, normally after they had reached the "age of reason"—seven years old—and they could be married when they reached puberty, legally set at age twelve.[5] Because of their value to the family as property to be traded, prospective wives were also often deprived of the opportunity to act as individuals, to come and go as they chose. Confined physically to safe places, places where they could not possibly encounter a man unattended, such women were preserved for the trade in marriage that would bring the greatest benefit to their families. Duby has also argued convincingly that, from the twelfth century onwards, the medieval church began to promote marriage in order to subdue and control the role of women, as well as to regularize male lines of inheritance.

While a medieval woman might very well have desired to marry, might have married a man whom she liked, loved, or respected, might have been treated well, and might have been a powerful force in her household or village, she normally did not enjoy the same political privileges and financial well-being granted her husband. In most instances the wealth she brought to marriage was controlled by her husband during the marriage, and could revert to her male relatives if she were widowed without having given birth to children.[6] In short, the state of marriage transformed a woman who could hold land and sue offenders into a woman who held no property whatsoever and enjoyed no legal status independent of her husband.

While Chaucer's portrayal of wives and prospective wives in all the *Tales* is beyond the scope of this study, it is my contention that Chaucer was particularly attuned to the roles medieval women were asked to perform by their society and to the ways in which these roles may have affected women themselves.⁷ That we can speak of the "women themselves" when referring to Chaucer's female characters—not to historical women—attests to a narrative trick practiced by Chaucer that may be explained in terms of Mikhail Bakhtin's notion of dialogic discourse.⁸

According to Bakhtin, readers of novelistic discourse interpret this discourse by analyzing the dialogical contact between an author and his or her characters.⁹ By discovering which character's voice is undercut and which is appropriated by the author, a reader may come to understand the author's discourse and intent. Bakhtin writes: "The author represents this language [of another], carries on a conversation with it, and the conversation penetrates into the interior of this language-image and dialogizes it from within."¹⁰ But in Chaucerian discourse, this bipartite relationship is overt in the relationship between Chaucer's narrators and the characters whose stories are told, while the author seems not to engage overtly in such dialogical contact. The narrators try so hard and so publicly to construct their tales that readers are apt to construe them as authors. The expected dialogical relationship is often transferred as a result from Chaucer and his characters onto Chaucer's narrators and the characters whose stories are told. The author's absence in this sense has the further effect of rendering Chaucer's characters seemingly independent of any authorial control, as Chaucer's narrators do not pretend to determine how their characters act and speak, but rather claim to follow an authority. Indeed, when Chaucer's narrators present characters speaking in indirect discourse, this discourse is heavily and overtly dialogized. But when these same characters speak in direct discourse, it is as though they have escaped the polemicizing voice of the narrator and are speaking to us directly. They seem to be living beings who could just as easily have said or done something different, and many readers tend to judge them in this way. Consider the case of Criseyde, criticized for behavior that is dictated by the story of Troy.¹¹

Chaucer encourages readers to assume that his characters can choose their own destiny. The assumption may be formalized in the statement: "She thinks apart from her narrator; she does not fit with the story he tells; therefore she exists." This illusion of freedom is important to feminist studies of Chaucer's work, as female voices intrude into male discourse and, more often than not, subvert the privileged narrative, if only temporarily. Chaucer's works thus reproduce in fiction male control over female experience and expression, *and* female voices objecting to that control. Encoded as the outbreak of unexpected female desires and attitudes within tales told by men, these voices confront the conventions of misogyny as well as the speakers of those conventions and, indeed, audiences schooled in misogynistic values.

Many of Chaucer's narrators parade their antifeminist values and many critics proclaim Geoffrey Chaucer a misogynist.[12] But the poems themselves question, attack, and undermine these values, often by the inclusion of female voices that do not mesh with the story at hand. Female voices threaten the power relationship inscribed in the text: Chaucer presents not only the stereotypes of women that promote misogyny, but also characters who do not fit those stereotypes. If we subtract the portraits of women created by male narrators from the voices that create those women in the works, and listen to what they say, not to what others say about them, we have an entirely different set of female characters. It is all an illusion, a sleight of hand on Chaucer's part, but it is an effective device for promoting antimisogynistic values, if not outright feminist ones, and for undermining misogynistic assumptions about how women should behave.

Emelye of the *Knight's Tale*, a character controlled by her brother-in-law Theseus as well as by her male narrator, unexpectedly presents us with the first instance of female dissatisfaction and dissent. Theseus's garden in the *Knight's Tale*, which Emelye inhabits, shares one wall with the prison tower confining Palamon and Arcite. Similarities between the two structures have been thoroughly detailed by V. A. Kolve; both imprison their inhabitants, serve as small enclosures within which one can only walk "up and doun" or "to and fro," and these phrases, repeated often in the tale, help to underscore the overwhelming sense of limitation and of set boundaries encountered by all of the Knight's characters, Theseus included, in their Boethian universe.[13]

But Emelye and other women in the tale experience more constraints than do the Knight's male characters. Emelye in particular cannot champion or contest her own future, as Palamon and Arcite do in battle and in the tournament; she does not have a hand in determining anyone else's future, as Theseus and Perotheus do. Emelye's inactivity has led many readers of the tale to dismiss her as a two-dimensional character, one who serves the Knight's plot as the object of male desire but who does not excite sympathy or empathy from Chaucer's readers.[14] Indeed, she most often serves as a commodity of exchange between men, an object captured by Theseus and then given as a reward to the winner of the tournament in order to mitigate the two knights' violent impulses. Susan Crane's assessment of Emelye as "an occasion for [romance] adventure" explains her passivity within the economy of the romance genre.[15]

The Knight also objectifies Emelye, as he narrates his story, comparing her with the spring beauty of the May morning on which she enters Theseus's garden early in the tale:

> Yclothed was she fressh, for to devyse:
> Hir yelow heer was broyded in a tresse
> Bihynde hir bak, a yerde long, I gesse.
> And in the gardyn, at the sonne upriste,
> She walketh up and doun, and as hire liste
> She gadereth floures, party white and rede,
> To make a subtil gerland for hire hede;
> And as an aungel hevenysshly she soong.   (I.1048–55)

While she is said to be "fairer" (I.1035) and "fressher" (I.1037) than nature itself, she inhabits the same realm as the lily, the rose, the spring, and the garden, and seems an additional ornament to Theseus's property on which she walks with her long, blonde braid and her angelic singing voice. In addition, the enclosed garden, the lily, and Emelye's virginal state recall the *hortus conclusus*, a locus of purity in the Song of Songs, and her angelic singing recalls descriptions of the earthly paradise. But her association in Palamon's mind with Venus, who is also depicted in a garden in the tale (I.1939), marks her appearance in this garden with erotic overtones as well. Indeed, men in the tale seem to be attracted to her because of her combination of innocence and unselfconscious sensuality. Her long braid, her beautiful clothes, her resemblance to the rose as much as to the lily (I.1039–40) combine to make her in the eyes of her male suitors and of her narrator desirable in very physical terms.[16] It is in her role as an available woman, alone in the garden, that "Emelye the shene" is first spotted by the imprisoned knights, Palamon and Arcite. While they too are prisoners of Theseus, they look down from their tower into the garden and in so doing violate the small measure of privacy Emelye enjoys.

The fine line between captor and guardian for Emelye and her sister, Ypolita, is most clearly illustrated by the tale's first acts: Theseus conquers the "regne of Femenye" (I.866) and marries the vanquished queen. For

Theseus and the Knight who tells his story, the close tie between war and marriage, between overcoming a people in battle and subduing a woman, is apparent in the sudden juxtaposition of the two acts. The Knight, claiming that he does not have the time to go into all the details, says:

> I wolde have toold yow fully the manere
> How wonnen was the regne of Femenye
> By Theseus and by his chivalrye;
> And of the grete bataille for the nones
> Bitwixen Atthenes and Amazones;
> And how asseged was Ypolita,
> The faire, hardy queene of Scithia;
> And of the feste that was at hir weddynge,
> And of the tempest at hir hoom-comynge.   (I.876–84)

The wedding feast follows so fast upon the siege of Ypolita that the wedding takes on the attributes of the battle: we can imagine in the space between lines 881 and 883 the violence of a marriage performed against a woman's will. In the compression of his *occupatio*, the Knight unwittingly suggests similarities between the actual battle against the Amazons and a conventional courtly battle for a woman's "mercy." Two aspects of the chivalric ideal, prowess in battle and prowess in love, come together in this image of a forced marriage.[17]

But the Knight does not intend to tell us about the siege of the Amazons, as "The remenant of the tale is long ynough" (I.888). So he begins his tale anew with the homecoming of Theseus ("I wol ayeyn bigynne" [I.892]). But here, too, the Knight's narrative dwells on the relationship between the powerful Theseus and powerless females, this time "A compaignye of ladyes, tweye and tweye" (I.898) who have lost their husbands to the villainy of Creon. Theseus again rises to the task and slays the evil Creon, thus allowing the ladies to care for their dead. The start of the tale, then, interlaces images of bloody battles with the needs of powerless women. In this context, Palamon and Arcite are found in a pile of dead bodies (I.1020), and just fifteen lines later (I.1035), Emelye wakes early one fine spring morning and prepares to do observance to May. The chivalric imperatives of violence and romance—for Theseus, Palamon, and Arcite—create a place for women that is both protective and porous. The enclosed garden where Emelye walks is at once her prison as a captured

Figure 6. Illustration from a manuscript of Giovanni Boccaccio's *Il Filostrato*, ca. 1455, French. Vienna, Natl. Lib. MS. 2617, fol. 53. Reprinted by permission of Bildarchiv der Österreichische Nationalbibliothek, Vienna.

female and her enclosed showcase as a marriageable virgin, and it symbolizes her protection from an outer world in which men do battle with great violence, at times ankle-deep in blood (I.1660).

Figure 6, from a fifteenth-century French manuscript of Boccaccio's *Teseida*, encapsulates all of these functions.[18] In it, Boccaccio's Emilia sits on a turf bench before a trellised wall of roses, a pose suggesting her affinity with nature's beauty and presenting her as a desirable object. The high brick wall that marks the far boundary of the garden keeps Emilia safe within the confines of her brother-in-law's castle. But at least two of the other three walls are porous, or are invisible in the picture. Palamon and Arcite gaze upon Emilia from their prison cell (not from the high tower Chaucer describes), and the viewer gazes freely at her from beyond the picture's frame, for only a very short trellis and a low brick planter separate us from Emilia. We can see much more of her, in fact, than her two would-be suitors can, since only the top of Emilia's head may be visible to the knights. As discussed in chapter 1, aristocratic pleasure gardens appear to have provided a space for decidedly social pastimes, and in literature when someone enters a garden alone, it is often so that he or she can be overheard. Emilia's sole occupation of the garden may signal her "resistance," in Susan Crane's formulation, to the social ties to which she will eventually acquiesce.[19]

In any case, the contrast between male and female worlds is encoded in Chaucer's poem in the contrast between this enclosed garden and the groves, forests, and open fields that frequently serve in the tale as *loci* for a variety of combative scenes between men. While Palamon and Arcite do not consider themselves free of the prison of love once they are freed from the prison tower, nevertheless they can and do ride out beyond the city's boundaries into the open fields and forests. When Arcite wishes to do observance to May, he rides out from the court into the field and on into the grove where Palamon is hiding:

> He on a courser, startlynge as the fir,
> Is riden into the feeldes hym to pleye,
> Out of the court, were it a myle or tweye.
> And to the grove of which that I yow tolde
> By aventure his wey he gan to holde.   (I.1502–6)

But when Emelye wishes to do observance to May early in the first book, she walks into Theseus's garden:

> This maked Emelye have remembraunce
> To doon honour to May, and for to ryse.   (I.1046–47)

> And in the gardyn, at the sonne upriste,
> She walketh up and doun, and as hire liste
> She gadereth floures, party white and rede,
> To make a subtil gerland for hire hede.   (I.1051–54)

Arcite, too, makes a garland of flowers from woodbine and hawthorn branches (I.1507–8), and while the basic form of both acts of spring observance match—in the search for a private outdoor setting and in the making of flowery garlands—the two *loci* are markedly different: Arcite's is open, Emelye's enclosed.[20]

This difference might not alone merit comment because it could simply attest to the social realities of Chaucer's contemporaries: women could not safely ride out into the countryside on their own (though Emelye and Ypolita do accompany Theseus on a hunting expedition), and a servant to the court could not find refuge in the castle's private garden. But in the context of Emelye's prayer to the goddess Diana, its symbolic significance emerges. Emelye herself realizes the physical constraints placed upon her by her role in Theseus's household, and she envisions an alternate future of being able to move freely into the open fields and forests beyond the city which, to her, represents a freedom from the marriage bond:

> Chaste goddesse, wel wostow that I
> Desire to ben a mayden al my lyf,
> Ne nevere wol I be no love ne wyf.
> I am, thow woost, yet of thy compaignye,
> A mayde, and love huntynge and venerye,
> And for to walken in the wodes wilde,
> And noght to ben a wyf and be with childe.
> Noght wol I knowe compaignye of man.   (I.2304–11)

Emelye proceeds to admit she may have to marry one or the other of her suitors. Still, she ends her prayer by reiterating her foremost desire:

> Bihoold, goddesse of clene chastitee,
> The bittre teeris that on my chekes falle.
> Syn thou art mayde and kepere of us alle,
> My maydenhede thou kepe and wel conserve,
> And whil I lyve, a mayde I wol thee serve.   (I.2326–30)

Emelye's desire to remain chaste underscores her identification with the Virgin and the enclosed garden of the Song of Songs. But in this context—that of a chivalric narrative—it is so inappropriate that it elicits no comment from the vast majority of critics of the tale. Until very recently, critics expressed a patronizing acknowledgement of her apparently childish wishes.[21] She does not want to know the company of a man, anathema to the chivalric notion of how women should behave. This is perhaps most forcefully represented in the goddess Diana's reaction to her prayer:

> But sodeynly she [Emelye] saugh a sighte queynte,
> For right anon oon of the fyres queynte,
> And quyked agayn, and after that anon
> That oother fyr was queynt and al agon.   (I.2333–36)

From the quenched torches run what appear to be drops of blood (I.2340), a graphic image of lost maidenhead following several puns on the female genitalia with the word "queynt[e]," meaning literally "curious" or "strange" as an adjective, "quench" or "go out" as a verb in the passage.[22] Then the goddess herself explains to Emelye that her prayer cannot be honored because of "eterne word written and confermed" (I.2350), adding: "Thou shalt ben wedded unto oon of tho / That han for thee so muchel care and wo" (I.2351–52). While "eterne word" indicates a divine plan, it is equally applicable to the Knight's narrative plan and Theseus's plan to marry her off. To Emelye, it hardly matters since the effect for her is the same. In short, male desire prevails, and because Palamon and Arcite have so much "care and wo," one of them will be rewarded with Emelye in marriage.

Some three hundred lines later, the Knight explains in an aside that all women are at Fortune's mercy: "(For wommen, as to speken in comune, / Thei folwen alle the favour of Fortune)" (I.2681–82). In addition to the misogynistic undertones of this comment—that women will do whatever they can to benefit themselves—in the context of Arcite's victory smile up at Emelye, it seems the Knight here acknowledges the extent to which women must obey the will of others. While Theseus admits that men, too, are ruled by destiny and a divine plan that belies human understanding, the tale itself seems to make a point of portraying Emelye and other women as even less free, more in thrall to the whims of Fortune than are their male counterparts. In the poem's exploration of free will and predestination, Emelye's case stands out. She does not even enjoy the appearance of free will. Palamon and Arcite, like Emelye, each choose which god to address in prayer before the tournament. But, unlike Emelye's, their prayers are heard and honored. Palamon wins Emelye with his prayer to Venus; Arcite wins the battle with his prayer to Mars. Only Emelye's prayer is flatly denied.

Further, the identification of Emelye with natural, seasonal rhythms not only emphasizes her role as ornamental object, but also underscores her imprisonment in this male-authored narrative. She cannot work against the seasonal rhythms; when the sun comes up, so must she: "Up roos the sonne, and up roos Emelye" (I.2272). When the spring sets forth its blossoms, she must also show her beauty. Not only is she contained in her brother-in-law's space, the enclosed garden, and in a chivalric romance told from a male perspective (we are meant to empathize with Palamon and Arcite), but her physical appearance and entrance into the tale is also created by a male voice—the Knight's. Indeed, the Knight's relationship to Emelye exhibits some of the same features that mark her relationship to Palamon and Arcite. He, too, seems fascinated by both her purity and her sensuality. In describing her preparation for prayer at the temple of Diana, the Knight observes:

> This Emelye, with herte debonaire,
> Hir body wessh with water of a welle.
> But hou she dide hir ryte I dar nat telle,
> But it be any thing in general;
> And yet it were a game to heeren al.
> To hym that meneth wel it were no charge;
> But it is good a man been at his large.
> Hir brighte heer was kembd, untressed al.   (I.2282–89)

The control the male narrator enjoys over his female character appears not only proprietary but also voyeuristic. He claims that he will not tell his audience all the details of her ablutions, though of course he could, but only indicate them in the most general terms. And yet, he cannot help but add that it would be fun to hear all about her bath, and he leaves each man "at his large," responsible for his own reading and imaging of this passage, a situation akin to that of the viewer in figure 6.

Theseus's garden in the *Knight's Tale* represents the way in which men control, guard, and imprison women for their own purposes: political, personal, and narrative. As wives or as prospective wives, women must be contained, this tale explains indirectly, because if left to their own devices women would live among themselves, like the Amazons, or in chaste service to Diana, as Emelye desires. Vulnerable to the cruelty of men like Creon, women require the protection that powerful men like Theseus can provide. But contradicting this *sentence* is the voice of Emelye, negating the desires imputed to her by the men of the tale. "Noght wol I knowe compaignye of man" (I.2311), she prays, and we glimpse an alternate life for her, a different potential narrative, one that might *not* be termed a "noble storie" by the "gentils everichon" (I.3111, 3113). Indeed, as the narratives of the pilgrimage accumulate, female voices become more frequent and, at times, much stronger than the male voices that seek to contain them.

Images of nature, many in conjunction with women, also abound in the *Merchant's Tale*. The heroine, May, shares with Emelye the distinction of being described by seasonal and natural images. While Emelye is "fressher than the May with floures newe" (I.1036), May is herself simply "fresshe May" (IV.1859, 1977, 2092, 2116), the metaphor made literal in her name. May's elderly husband, January, uses the spring image of a blossoming fruit tree to describe himself and his ongoing sexual desire, further claiming that his limbs can be compared to the evergreen laurel tree, never aging:

> Thogh I be hoor, I fare as dooth a tree
> That blosmeth er that fruyt ywoxen bee;
> And blosmy tree nys neither drye ne deed.
> I feele me nowhere hoor but on myn heed;
> Myn herte and alle my lymes been as grene
> As laurer thurgh the yeer is for to sene.   (IV.1461–66)

The phrase "alle my lymes" seems to refer not only to January's arms and legs, but to his phallus as well, since he defines his vitality in sexual terms.

In addition, January's vision of marriage as a paradise takes the pervasive spring image of the tale and codifies it into a permanent state. Paradise enjoys eternal spring, and January seems to think not only that wedlock is a paradisal and permanent experience, but a man's wife is herself her husband's paradise on earth: "'Noon oother lyf', seyde he, 'is worth a bene, / For wedlok is so esy and so clene, / That in this world it is a paradys' (IV.1263–65).... 'That wyf is mannes helpe and his confort, / His paradys terrestre, and his disport'" (IV.1331–32). January believes that nothing but good will issue from the "sacrament" of marriage (IV.1319). Indeed, once married to May, he exclaims gleefully: "A man may do no synne with his wyf" (IV.1839), an erroneous notion since the church strictly regulated marital intercourse.

Others in the tale do not share January's vision of marriage, including Theophrastus, whom January quotes, and January's advisor Justinus. In fact, Justinus argues that a good servant is a far better companion than a wife, as a wife may become a man's purgatory on earth, not his paradise (IV.1670), contradicting January's image of a permanent spring with one of lengthy strife. Justinus cites the Wife of Bath as one of his authorities on all the "wo that is in mariage" (III.3), alluding not only to the Wife's own troubles but to the troubles she presumably brings to a husband. Indeed, May proves an imperfect wife. Until the wedding night, she is an idealized, beautiful, young woman either imagined or seen from a distance. But as soon as the matrimonial bonds are finalized and the two are left together in bed, we discover that May has desires, likes, and dislikes of her own. Up to this point, January presents himself in his own terms—white-haired but as green as a laurel tree and full of sexual energy. When May enters the tale as a separate individual, a second picture of January as a husband emerges. May is brought to his bed "as stille as stoon" (IV.1817), and she seems not to enjoy the first night of lovemaking with her new husband as much as he seems to. While he "was al coltissh, ful of ragerye" (IV.1847) and "laboureth he til that the day gan dawe" (IV.1842), May "preyseth nat his pleyyng worth a bene" (IV.1854). In addition, May keeps to her room for three days afterwards, presumably to rest from the exertion of their night of passion, though the valence of these lines in context suggests that she is repulsed by January and wishes to remain separated from him for as long as she can.

This bifurcated perspective of the marriage may be traced to Chaucer's use of two distinct sources.[23] In one, Eustache Deschamps' *Miroir de Mariage*, an old man, Franc Vouloir, seeks advice on marriage from his friends. Several false friends urge marriage for several of the reasons put forth by January in Chaucer's version, and Franc Vouloir imagines a young wife, fifteen to twenty years old, who will care for him as he ages, work hard, talk little, and bear him children who will remember him after his death. Franc Vouloir's faithful friend Repertoire de Science, however, advises against marriage to a young woman for many of the same reasons put forth by Justinus and Theophrastus in the *Merchant's Tale*. But nowhere is the woman's point of view represented. In a second source, Boccaccio's *Ameto*, a young nymph, Agape, narrates the story of her marriage to a wealthy old man. She describes her husband's white hair, his prickly beard, and the loose, wrinkled skin on his neck, among other things, which echo the description of January on his wedding night (IV.1824–25, 1849). While May in the *Merchant's Tale* does not herself describe January in these terms, the narrator does once May has entered the tale and brought with her a second perspective. Further, Boccaccio's Agape complains that her husband cannot make love to her but keeps her up all night trying, and, like May, she finally finds happiness with a younger man. In the *Merchant's Tale*, these two perspectives clash as Franc Vouloir meets Agape: his imagined paradise is her actual hell. But it is only in Chaucer's version that the narrative progresses until *her* paradise becomes *his* hell. Indeed, much of the tale's comedy derives from the inversion of several elements, not the least of which is the traditional power relationship between an elderly, landowning male and a young female commoner who finally gains the upper hand. This inversion is also played out in the tale's garden imagery.

Three distinct garden *topoi* figure prominently in the *Merchant's Tale*, and each one is inverted by the end of the tale as the narrative associated with each *topos* undergoes a significant transformation. The *paradys d'amours*, associated with the *Roman de la Rose* and the male lover's conquest of the object of his desire, appears first in the tale when the Merchant compares January's pleasure garden with the garden of the *Roman de la Rose*:

> He made a gardyn, walled al with stoon;
> So fair a gardyn woot I nowher noon.
> For, out of doute, I verraily suppose
> That he that wroot the Romance of the Rose
> Ne koude of it the beautee wel devyse;
> Ne Priapus ne myghte nat suffise,
> Though he be god of gardyns, for to telle
> The beautee of the gardyn and the welle
> That stood under a laurer alwey grene.   (IV.2029–37)

While the Merchant does not describe the garden in detail—we know only that a stone wall encloses it and that inside the garden a laurel tree shades a well—we are invited to imagine a garden as beautiful and as sensuous as the one described in the *Roman*. The reference to Priapus underscores the erotic purpose of this garden as does the reference to the *Roman*'s well of Narcissus in which the dreamer of the *Roman* first sees his beloved, the rose, and is seized by desire for it.[24] In addition, Pluto and Proserpine dance about January's well:

> Ful ofte tyme he Pluto and his queene,
> Proserpina, and al hire fayerye,
> Disporten hem and maken melodye
> Aboute that welle, and daunced, as men tolde.   (IV.2038–41)

Like January, the elderly and powerful Pluto plays in the garden with his young and beautiful wife. Further, the phrase "laurer alwey grene" recalls the description January gives himself earlier in the poem, suggesting that he will preside over this garden much like the pine tree shading the *Roman*'s well of Narcissus.[25] But it also recalls January's hoary head of the preceding descriptive passage—his old age—and points to a crucial difference between January's pleasure garden and the garden of the *Roman*. In the *Roman*, Old Age appears to be excluded from entering the garden, along with such other undesirables as Hatred, Covetousness, Avarice, Envy, Hypocrisy, and Poverty.[26] January's garden, however, fashioned after the *Roman*, has a wall meant to exclude the younger men January has reason to fear. Especially apprehensive once he has lost his sight, January forces May to remain with him constantly:

> That neither in halle, n'yn noon oother hous,
> Ne in noon oother place, neverthemo,
> He nolde suffre hire for to ryde or go,
> But if that he had hond on hire alway.   (IV.2088–91)

January has made May his prisoner if not his servant, and the presence of Pluto and Proserpine in January's garden underscores January's treatment of May as unfair.[27] Chaucer would have known several versions of the Pluto-Proserpine story, including Ovid's in *Metamorphoses* 5 and Claudian's incomplete version in his poem *De raptu Proserpinae*, mentioned in passing in the *Merchant's Tale* (IV.2232). Both stories concur in Pluto's use of force in abducting Proserpine and both texts present a female perspective of the event. In Ovid's version, the nymph Cyane voices her outrage at the abduction and rape to Pluto: "non potes invitae Cereris gener esse: roganda, / non rapienda fuit . . ." (V.415–16) [You cannot be Ceres' son-in-law against her will; the girl should have been asked, not seized]. Cyane, however, soon dissolves in tears and becomes water in the pool of Palici, thus losing the ability to complain further or help Ceres to find her daughter. Ovid's passage also contrasts the cool pond and flowering grove where Proserpine plays to the sulphurous, boiling pools at hell's entrance, thus heightening the contrast between the bountiful earth of Proserpine's youth and the barren depths of Pluto's realm, as well as emphasizing the abrupt change Proserpine experiences. In addition, Ovid's version of the story is driven by female desire for power. Venus desires control over Pluto's third of the world just as she has conquered the upper two-thirds with Cupid's help, so she orders Cupid to take aim at Pluto. Pluto sees Proserpine and falls in love with her.

In Claudian's version, three goddesses—Venus, Diana, and Pallas Athena—are enlisted by Jove to help in the abduction, and they entice Proserpine from her mother's iron palace on Sicily into a paradisal spring landscape. When Pluto arrives to seize her—in this version he wants a wife without having been shot by Cupid's arrow—the three goddesses try to prevent Pluto from taking Proserpine. A thunderbolt from Jove curtails their subversive activity, but as Proserpine leaves in Pluto's chariot, she rails at her father, Jove, for devising such a fate for her. In both versions, Proserpine is taken from a paradisal spot—Ovid describes a Mediterranean *locus amoenus* (V.388–91); Claudian embellishes his lush spot with a catalogue of trees (II.107–11).

The association of January's garden with Pluto and Proserpine underscores May's probable reluctance to marry January as well as the extent to which she may have been forced into the arrangement. From what little we are told of the affair, it seems to be a matter of legal paperwork that not only makes May a wife but also enfeoffs her to January's estate.[28] The details of the transaction are hastily glossed over just as the transaction itself happens quickly:

> For whan they [Justinus and his brother] saughe that it moste
>   nedes be,
> They wroghten so, by sly and wys tretee,
> That she, this mayden which that Mayus highte,
> As hastily as evere that she myghte
> Shal wedded be unto this Januarie.
> I trowe it were to longe yow to tarie,
> If I yow tolde of every scrit and bond
> By which that she was feffed in his lond,
> Or for to herknen of hir riche array.   (IV.1691–99)

May, previously described as "a mayden in the toun / . . . of smal degree" (IV.1623–25), has somehow been sold or traded into matrimony with the wealthy old landowner.

January's garden, associated initially with the pleasure park of the *Roman*, with the fertility god Priapus, and with the abduction of Proserpine, thus concretizes both January's desire for erotic pleasure with his young wife and that young wife's distaste for the entire arrangement, as someone who, like Proserpine, has been forced into the marriage. When May falls in love with the young courtier Damyan and plots to meet him secretly in January's garden, she successfully wrests control over her own sexual pleasure from January, first by counterfeiting the key to the garden gate and then by tricking January with her desire to pick pears. May's counterfeiting the key to the garden gate by using hot wax recalls January's desire to marry a young woman he could mold like wax to his own specifications, so May appropriates January's image of pliant wax as well as his garden. The quintessentially male pleasure park is thus inverted by May, made to serve her own passion, and because of the strong connection to Proserpine, May seems at least partly justified in her actions.[29]

The narratives associated with two biblical gardens are also inverted in the tale. January's erotic love song to May uses many lines from the Vulgate version of the Song of Songs, as summarized below:

Rys up, my wyf, my love, my lady free! (IV.2138)
[surge propera amica mea formonsa mea et veni (2:10)]
The turtles voys is herd, my dowve sweete (IV.2139)
[vox turturis audita est (2:12) . . . columba mea (2:14)]
The wynter is goon with alle his reynes weete (IV.2140)
[iam enim hiemps transiit imber abiit et recessit (2:11)]
Com forth now, with thyne eyen columbyn! (IV.2141)
[ecce tu pulchra oculi tui columbarum (1:14)]
How fairer been thyn brestes than is wyn! (IV.2142)
[quam pulchrae sunt mammae tuae . . . pulchriora ubera tua vino (4:10)]
The gardyn is enclosed al aboute (IV.2143)
[hortus conclusus soror mea sponsa hortus conclusus fons signatus (4:12)]
Com forth my white spouse! Out of doute (IV.2144)
[dilectus meus candidus (5:10)]
Thou hast me wounded in myn herte, O wyf! (IV.2145)
[vulnerasti cor meum soror mea sponsa (4:9)]
No spot of thee ne knew I al my lyf (IV.2146)
[tota pulchra es amica mea et macula non est in te (4:7)]

Close parallels and echoes both in syntax and in imagery give way, however, to the old husband's final two lines, which have no parallel whatsoever in the Song of Songs: "Com forth, and lat us taken oure disport; / I chees thee for my wyf and my confort" (IV.2147–48). Like Pluto, January uses the garden for "disport," and he has perverted the meaning of the Latin text by interpreting the biblical lyric erotically. The imagery of the garden, of going to the garden, of partaking of each other's gardens alludes solely to erotic pleasure. January's misreading and misuse of the Song of Songs illustrates the dangers inherent in an undirected or untutored reading of the Bible.[30] January's perversion points up his use of various conventional texts in self-serving ways. Like Alison of Bath, January interprets St. Paul's instruction that "it is better to marry than to burn" (1 Corinthians 7:9) as a license for physical pleasure.[31]

Thus January's misreading of the Song of Songs inverts a holy lyric about chaste and holy love into a song about lust and erotic desire, as May's usurpation of the garden associated with the *Roman de la Rose* inverts a narrative of male desire and acquisition into one of female desire and the power to fulfill that desire. Similarly, the narrative scene in the tale associated with the Garden of Eden provides a third example of comic inversion.[32] At the tale's climax, the three characters gathered about the pear tree resemble in their roles Adam, Eve, and the serpent in the Garden of Eden. If May represents Eve, the pear tree the tree of the knowledge of good and evil, and Damyan the serpent, then January must be Adam. But if January is Adam, then he should be invited by May to share in the pleasure of the pear tree, and, as a result of her action, May should be punished with pain. In the *Merchant's Tale*, however, May is rewarded with illicit pleasure with Damyan that remains unpunished in the tale. The final effect of this tale differs fundamentally from the biblical narrative.[33] Admittedly, the Merchant's is an amoral world driven by the pleasure-seeking principle. But it is significant that the wife succeeds in subverting her husband's control over her and that her success in overturning the expected power relationship drives the comedy of the tale.

The *Merchant's Tale* has often been read as a bitter comedy, since the Merchant, like January, seems to have been deceived by a young wife. But as is the case with exempla in many works, the teller of the tale may not himself be fully aware of, or fully in control of, his exemplary narrative.[34] In this tale, women fight back at their oppressors—Proserpine prevails over Pluto when she provides May with the proper retort at the moment January regains his sight, and May, also trapped in a forced marriage, beats January at his own sexual game. Indeed, January, May, and the Merchant himself are all engaged in misreading and inverting the conventional narratives associated with three garden *topoi*: the *paradys d'amours*, the *hortus conclusus*, and the Garden of Eden. Proserpine's question to Pluto—"What rekketh me of youre auctoritees?" (IV.2276)—is essentially what January has said to Justinus regarding marriage, what May has said to January regarding her role in the marriage, and what the Merchant has said to his audience regarding the outcome of the story of the Fall of Man and the "sorwe and care" (IV.1228) that women, not men, are supposed to suffer. At the story's climactic moment, May becomes, in a sense, both Proserpine and Eve as she is pulled up into the pear tree: "And caughte hire by a twiste, and up she gooth—" (IV.2349). In her collusion with the serpent figure, she reënacts the Fall of Man. But at the same time, being lifted up from January's garden-prison, May resembles Proserpine escaping from Pluto and the underworld for part of the year.

Despite the efforts of generations of critics, there can be no simple moral to this tale. In tales analogous to the pear tree episode, St. Peter and the Lord restore the blind husband's sight. Chaucer replaces St. Peter and the Lord with Pluto and Proserpine. In so doing, he also converts a text for his own purposes. It is my contention that his purposes involve, at least in part, demonstrating how one woman—May—challenges and revises the role assigned her by her culture.

Another tale that involves a woman and a garden is the *Franklin's Tale*, which pits two courtly narratives, both involving the same woman, against one another. The tale begins when a knight, Arveragus, falls in love with a lady, Dorigen. In the space of twenty lines he does service to her and she accepts him as her husband. The Franklin's extended meditation on their relationship as a perfect love match claims that the knight is his lady's servant in love and her master in marriage, an arrangement Kittredge also thought the perfect culmination to the marriage group:[35] "Heere may men seen an humble, wys accord; / Thus hath she take hir servant and hir lord,— / Servant in love, and lord in mariage" (V.791–93). Although the Franklin also speaks against "maistrye," saying that women "desiren libertee, / And nat to been constreyned as a thral" (V.768–69), he sees no contradiction in the husband's position as lord of his wife in a legal sense and his wife's presumed desire for liberty. Indeed, the match appears perfect. Dorigen loves Arveragus "as hire hertes lyf" (V.816), and Arveragus takes her home to Brittany where he "lyveth in blisse and in solas" (V.802). In just seventy lines, then, the Franklin has told an entire story of married love and alluded to its pleasures.

The narrative begins anew, however, when Arveragus decides to leave his wife of about a year to go to England "To seke in armes worshipe and honour" (V.811), leaving Dorigen in an extreme state of grief: "She moorneth, waketh, wayleth, fasteth, pleyneth" (819). With her friends' help, Dorigen is eventually distracted from her grief as they spend a day in the castle's garden:

> They goon and pleye hem al the longe day.
> And this was on the sixte morwe of May,
> Which May hadde paynted with his softe shoures
> This gardyn ful of leves and of floures;
> And craft of mannes hand so curiously
> Arrayed hadde this gardyn, trewely,
> That nevere was ther gardyn of swich prys
> But if it were the verray paradys.   (V.905–12)

This May garden resembles several examined above; a pleasure park, a *paradys d'amours*, and compared with the earthly paradise, it is used by Dorigen's friends to lift her spirits and to indulge in their own pastimes. A relatively private space in which the members of the upper class could spend their leisure time, this garden sits on one side of Arveragus's castle. On the other side is the rough coast of Brittany, so the castle itself separates the rocky coast, which causes Dorigen to fear for her husband's safe return, from the garden, which provides her with some interim pleasure.

But what distinguishes this garden from others we have seen in Chaucer's *Tales* is the mention of human effort in producing the desired effect. As is noted in chapter 3, the narrator's description of Criseyde's garden also emphasizes the role of human effort in producing the effects. Nevertheless, this remains an unusual focus in descriptions of ideal gardens. A large part of most comparisons of literary gardens with the earthly paradise arises from the sense that the garden grows perfectly without human intervention. But Arveragus's garden is "arrayed" "curiously" by the "craft of mannes hand," and as such is presented as a consciously created space, not one that appears to grow in such a way naturally.

In addition, the garden is said to be so lovely that anyone in it should be happy, unless sick or in great distress:

> The odour of floures and the fresshe sighte
> Wolde han maked any herte lighte
> That evere was born, but if to greet siknesse
> Or to greet sorwe helde it in distresse,
> So ful it was of beautee with plesaunce. (V.913–17)

Dorigen seems not to qualify as one who is too sick or too anxiety-ridden to enjoy the garden. While sad not to see her husband among the dancers, she eventually allows her grief to subside:

> For she ne saugh hym on the daunce go
> That was hir housbonde and hir love also.
> But nathelees she moste a tyme abyde
> And with good hope lete hir sorwe slyde. (V.921–24)

Dorigen is comforted by the crafted beauty of her husband's pleasure garden, a space that alludes to the world of love's pleasures, a world Dorigen has presumably known with her husband, who is "hir love also," and who is never far from her thoughts.

But in this pleasure park a young squire, Aurelius, spots Dorigen, whom he has admired from a distance, and he takes the opportunity to speak with her, thus complicating the Franklin's plot considerably. From the introduction of Aurelius onwards, the tale presents a conflict between married love and courtly love situated in the character of Dorigen. That the squire approaches Dorigen in the garden underscores our sense that the garden is designed and intended for love-games.[36] That she acknowledges his presence and speaks with him makes her a willing participant in the game of courtesy. Dorigen in fact continues to think primarily of her husband while participating in banter with Aurelius, so that when she says, "in pley" (V.988), that she would consider rewarding his advances if he could remove the black rocks that threaten her husband's journey home, she maintains her role as devoted wife even as she becomes a lady involved in courtly conversation with a "lusty squier" (V.937). Thus the pleasure park that reminds her of her absent husband becomes also the site of a second suitor's advance, and as such represents the conflicting roles Dorigen is called upon to perform in the tale: dutiful wife and unescorted courtly lady.

This conflict between married love, that of Dorigen and Arveragus, and courtly love, felt only by Aurelius, reaches its crisis with the apparent disappearance of the black rocks, long after Arveragus has returned safely from England. Dorigen feels trapped when Aurelius confronts her with her former promise. He recalls the earlier situation by referring to the place itself: "But in a gardyn yond, at swich a place, / Ye woot right wel what ye bihighten me" (V.1326–27). The garden has come to symbolize to him their agreement, made "in pley" by Dorigen but taken seriously by Aurelius. Dorigen, horrified at this turn of events, "astoned stood" (V.1339) once Aurelius has left her:

> In al hir face nas a drope of blood.
> She wende nevere han come in swich a trappe.
> "Allas," quod she, "that evere this sholde happe!
> For wende I nevere by possibilitee
> That swich a monstre or merveille myghte be!
> It is agayns the proces of nature." (V.1340–45)

Like the garden itself, crafted "by mannes hand," the rocks' disappearance has been crafted by the magician from Orleans, with some assistance from the tides; Dorigen's words to Aurelius have been crafted to mean something other than she meant when she uttered them, and Dorigen's own craftiness in play with Aurelius returns to haunt her, a happily married woman.[37]

But is Dorigen at fault for her participation in verbal play with Aurelius? Considered in the context of the *paradys d'amours*, Dorigen's words "in pley" conform to the conventions of courtly love as satirized by Andreas Capellanus in his dialogues. Dorigen's second answer to Aurelius's plea resembles those given in Andreas's work by women who would prefer not to be bothered by unwanted suitors. In the dialogue between a man of the middle class and a woman of the nobility, for example, the woman first gives an unequivocal answer to the man's plea for her love. Claiming that the class distinction is insurmountable, she tells the man:

"et si nullius sim amoris vinculo colligata, tu tamen quasi alienigena indignus meo reperiris amore" [though I am bound by no man's love, you are an alien, so to say, and so adjudged unworthy of my love].[38] Further along in their debate, the man says:

> Quamvis tuus me sermo depellat, quam diu tamen vixero a tui amoris proposito non recedam, quia etsi meae cogitationis fructum non sim percepturus spes tamen sola, quam ex mei ipsius cordis mera liberalitate assumpsi, meum faciet corpus tranquillam ducere vitam, et subsequenter forte Deus mei doloris tuae menti inseret remedium.

> [In spite of your dismissive words, I shall not abandon my designs on your love as long as I live. Even if I shall obtain no reward for my project, the mere hope which pure generosity of heart has caused me to entertain will make my body lead an undisturbed life. Later, perhaps, God will accomplish in your mind the remedy for my grief.][39]

The woman retorts: "Tuo Deus labori digna praemia ferat" [May God bring you rewards worthy of your toil], in which the suitor finds hope:

> Hoc solum verbum mihi spem indicat fructuosam, sed et ego Deum rogo ut semper tibi sit meae cura solutis, et mea vela quietis portum inveniant.

> [These are your only words which suggest I have a hope of success. But I ask God that you may ever have regard for my salvation, and that my sails may obtain the harbour of rest.][40]

Thus, as is frequent in Andreas's work, the man has the last word, and the woman who might have thought that her response was unambiguously negative finds herself the continuing object of her unwanted suitor's desire by virtue of his clever, self-interested interpretation of her words. Such is often the case in Andreas's dialogues since the author is at pains to demonstrate how a man can usually get what he wants from a woman if he makes the proper advance.

Similarly, Aurelius takes Dorigen's jest in earnest, and what she seems to have considered a friendly and clever retort following her unequivocally negative response, Aurelius has taken literally and seriously. In another context, Eugene Vance has discussed the firm line distinguishing jest from serious speech and lying in medieval philosophy. Citing St. Augustine in particular, Vance argues:

> To the extent that love is a mere game, its manifestation in language is innocent: medieval speculations upon lying were careful to exonerate deception perpetrated in play and jokes, which, according to St. Augustine (*De mendacio* ii.2; iii.3), are clearly distinct from lying.[41]

Indeed, one may wonder that Dorigen has been labeled a perpetrator of literal reading—of the letter that kills—by Chaucerians;[42] rather, it is Aurelius who misinterprets the tone and intent of Dorigen's jest and holds her to the literal fulfillment of her playful promise.

In addition, the perfection of the marriage between Dorigen and Arveragus is questionable. Arveragus, absent during much of the tale, not only leaves Dorigen to fend for herself with unwanted suitors such as Aurelius, but he also commands her to keep her promise to Aurelius in the tale's second act of extreme literalism. His strained definition of "trouthe," which involves the adultery of his wife, places a premium on appearances at the expense of Dorigen's lived experience and her "trouthe," or honorable behavior. He tells her: "Ye shul youre trouthe holden, by my fay!" (V.1474), and then explains:

> "Trouthe is the hyeste thyng that man may kepe"—
> But with that word he brast anon to wepe,
> And seyde, "I yow forbede, up peyne of deeth,
> That nevere, while thee lasteth lyf ne breeth,
> To no wight telle thou of this aventure." (V.1479–83)

"Trouthe" is here defined only as the keeping of a promise, not the telling of what is true or the exercise of honorable behavior, both meanings attested in Chaucer's works. In holding to just one meaning of "trouthe," Arveragus violates the other two meanings of the word. He commands his wife not only to tell lies to conceal what she is about to do, but the act of adultery itself, albeit condoned by him, contradicts codes of honorable intent and behavior in marriage.

A tale of crafted surface appearances, underlying realities, and the difficulty of knowing the difference, the *Franklin's Tale* abounds with characters, things, and events that are not as they seem. Arveragus pretends to be his wife's servant in love but he acts her master in all situations; Aurelius appears to be intent on courtly game with Dorigen but in fact presses his case in earnest; the garden where this game takes place seems distanced from worldly cares, separated from the rocky coast by Arveragus's castle, but it turns out to be the place of extreme crisis for the tale's heroine, taking the place of the black rocks she originally feared. The transformation of the *paradys d'amours* into the *locus* of a courtly crisis constitutes a "trappe" for Dorigen—she played the game as she thought she was expected to, but is then held to her jestful promise by both men in the tale. When she exclaims of the rocks' disappearance that it is "agayns the proces of nature" (V.1345), she voices the dilemma also posed by her husband's demand: it is "agayns the proces of nature" for a loving husband to order his wife into an adulterous relationship that, incidentally, could become the grounds for his repudiation of her if he chose to press the case with church authorities.[43]

At the tale's conclusion, the Franklin turns his story into the *questioni d'amore* found in Chaucer's source, Boccaccio's *Il Filocolo*. He asks: "Which was the mooste fre, as thynketh yow?" (V.1622), to which scholars have answered, variously, the husband, the lover, and the magician. All can be seen to display magnanimity and generosity, if not nobility.[44] Still, the question begs a second question if "fre" is read as "free" or "unrestricted," meanings also attested in Chaucer's work. If we can point to one or another of the male characters as "mooste fre" in this sense, too, as most free to travel to England to fight or to Orleans to visit a magician, can we not also point out that Dorigen is by far the least free, the most restricted character in the tale? Priscilla Martin, too, wonders about Dorigen in response to the question of generosity posed at the tale's end. She writes: "I find myself asking 'Who was the least free?' and, despite the vows of service made to her throughout the poem, answer 'Dorigen'."[45] While the *Franklin's Tale* does not present a version of female paradise, as I have argued the *Knight's* and *Merchant's Tales* do, it nevertheless demonstrates at least as clearly the limits to female activity in a fictional world created and governed by men. In the *Franklin's Tale,* this world is not only made up of male ideas regarding the perfect marriage and male ideas regarding a good narrative, but it is also governed by male ideas about courtly love—those of Andreas Capellanus and the character of Aurelius. These ideas dictate courtly behavior to Dorigen at the same time as they treat that conventional behavior as the expression of Dorigen's own emotional state and intentions in matters of love. It is "Swich a trappe" Dorigen finds herself in, ruled by conventions designed to make her fit the designs of men.

The garden of Dorigen's promise makes literal and visible the conventional role that defines her. As in Criseyde's case, convention—represented spatially by the garden—exerts pressure on Dorigen and when she acquiesces to that pressure, convention defines her as well. This study began by asserting that the spaces we create also influence us, signaling to us expected modes of behavior that can then be followed or resisted. Over the course of his literary career, Chaucer both demonstrates the power of conventions to control individual action and provides examples of resistance to that power. Such a vision seems to me a useful corrective to studies that emphasize only the influence of cultural imperatives on individual behavior. At the inception of the early modern period in Britain, in a literature that is at once dependent on poetic tradition and independent from it, Chaucer's vision of the individual in relation to social and literary conventions articulates a creative tension that his poetry enacts for us still. From the gardens of classical and medieval literature, and from the gardens and large pleasure parks of Chaucer's contemporaries, Chaucer fashions his own poetic gardens. As I hope I have demonstrated, Chaucer's use of convention requires close attention, for it is never as simple as it first appears.

Notes

Introduction

1. All quotations from Chaucer are taken from Larry D. Benson, ed., *The Riverside Chaucer*.
2. I take these quotations from Pearsall, ed., *The Floure and the Leafe, The Assembly of Ladies, The Isle of Ladies*.
3. Giamatti, *The Earthly Paradise*, p. 6.
4. Comito, *The Idea of the Garden*, p. xii.
5. Stewart, *The Enclosed Garden*, pp. xiii–xiv.
6. Giamatti, *The Earthly Paradise*, pp. 48–49.
7. Comito, *The Idea of the Garden*, p. xi.
8. Ibid., p. 152.
9. See especially Harvey, *Mediaeval Gardens*.
10. Deschamps, *Oeuvres*, 2: 139; Burrow, ed. and trans., *Geoffrey Chaucer: A Critical Anthology*, pp. 26, 28.
11. Gallo, ed. and trans., *The Poetria Nova*, p. 18.
12. Walsh, *Andreas Capellanus on Love*, p. 100.
13. Ibid., p. 101.
14. Ibid., p. 100.
15. Ibid., p. 101.
16. Gallo, *The Poetria Nova*, pp. 18–19.
17. De Certeau, *The Practice of Everyday Life*, pp. 97–98; quoting E. Benveniste.
18. Ibid., p. 97.
19. See Taylor, *Chaucer Reads "The Divine Comedy,"* p. 206.
20. Pound, *ABC of Reading*, p. 36.
21. Ibid., p. 36.
22. See, for example, Huppé and Robertson, *Fruyt and Chaf: Studies in Chaucer's Allegories*, pp. 110–17; Kee, "Two Chaucerian Gardens"; Kaske, "The

Canticum Canticorum in the *Miller's Tale*"; and Heffernan, "Wells and Streams in Three Chaucerian Gardens."

23. Jauss, *Toward an Aesthetic of Reception*, p. 88.

24. Chaucer's gardens may also draw on so-called "natural symbolism," as defined by historical geographers (see, for example, Appleton, *The Experience of Landscape*, and Cosgrove, *Social Formation and Symbolic Landscape*), but such an analysis is beyond the scope of this study.

Chapter 1

1. Dahlberg, trans., *The Romance of the Rose*, pp. 333, 337.

2. Pearsall and Salter, *Landscapes and Seasons*, p. 94. For opinions on the garden and park, see, for example, Comito, *The Idea of the Garden*, pp. 89–147; Smith, "In Search of the Ideal Landscape"; Baumgartner, "The Play of Temporalities"; and Hult, "Language and Dismemberment."

3. Pearsall and Salter, *Landscapes and Seasons*, p. 94.

4. Curtius, *European Literature and the Latin Middle Ages*, p. 195. See also Pearsall and Salter, *Landscapes and Seasons*, pp. 3–24, on the classical tradition.

5. Curtius, *European Literature and the Latin Middle Ages*, p. 195.

6. In his more general and far-reaching assessment of descriptions of classical gardens and blessed spots, Giamatti identifies many more authors who contributed to the wealth of the literary tradition of garden and nature description that medieval and Renaissance authors inherited (*The Earthly Paradise and the Renaissance Epic*, especially pp. 15–47). See also Pearsall and Salter, *Landscapes and Seasons*, pp. 47–53.

7. Curtius, *European Literature and the Latin Middle Ages*, p. 197.

8. Faral, *Les Arts Poétiques*, p. 149; Galyon, trans., *The Art of Versification*, p. 60.

9. See Giamatti, pp. 67–83; Bennett, *The Parlement of Foules: An Interpretation*, p. 70; and Pearsall and Salter, *Landscapes and Seasons*, pp. 56–75.

10. Giamatti, *The Earthly Paradise*, p. 15.

11. Ibid., pp. 70–71.

12. E. V. Gordon, ed., *Pearl*, p. 5.

13. See Luttrell, "*Pearl*: Symbolism in a Garden Setting," for a discussion of the Middle English terms *erber* and *huyle* as they are used in the poem.

14. Cited in Giamatti, *The Earthly Paradise*, p. 50. See Claudian, trans. Platnauer, pp. 246–49, lines 46–96.

15. Bennett, *The Parlement of Foules*, p. 80. See Statius, *Silvae*, I.ii.51–64.

16. Giamatti, *The Earthly Paradise*, p. 60.

17. See Matter, *The Voice of My Beloved*, p. 154; Daley, "The 'Closed Garden' and the 'Sealed Fountain,'" pp. 255–78; and Stewart, *The Enclosed Garden*, pp. 31–45.

18. Matter, *The Voice of My Beloved*, pp. 162–63.
19. See the discussion of *paradys d'amours* in Kee, pp. 156–58.
20. Ovid, *Metamorphoses* 10.90–108; Statius, *Thebaid*, VI.98–106; Claudian, *De raptu Proserpinae* II.107–11; Joseph of Exeter, *Iliad* I.505–10.
21. Curtius, *European Literature and the Latin Middle Ages*, pp. 194–95.
22. See especially Statius, *Thebaid*, book VI, lines 98–106.
23. Dahlberg, *The Romance of the Rose*, p. 49.
24. See Smith, "In Search of the Ideal Landscape," pp. 228–30.
25. Quintilian, V.10,20. Quintilian distinguishes between common-places, *loci communes*, and the places (also *loci*) where one could search for arguments specific to an individual case.
26. Curtius, *European Literature and the Latin Middle Ages*, p. 70.
27. Carruthers, *The Book of Memory*, p. 29. See also Comito, *The Idea of the Garden*, pp. 71–75.
28. Carruthers, *The Book of Memory*, p. 33.
29. Ibid., p. 33.
30. Ibid., p. 180.
31. Carruthers, "Poet as Master Builder," p. 887.
32. Translated from *De vegetabilibus et plantis*, Lib. VII, Tractatus I, cap. xiv, by Harvey, *Mediaeval Gardens*, p. 6.
33. For example, Harvey identifies Chaucer's and Froissart's fascination with the daisy as a love of the flower itself (*Mediaeval Gardens*, p. 131), without acknowledging the existence of the genre of *Marguerite* poetry so popular with Chaucer's French contemporaries (see Wimsatt, *The Marguerite Poetry of Guillaume de Machaut*).
34. Harvey, *Mediaeval Gardens*, p. 11.
35. Pearsall and Salter, *Landscapes and Seasons*, p. 110.
36. Translated by Calkins, "Piero de' Crescenzi and the Medieval Garden," pp. 172–73.
37. Ibid., p. 172; Curtius, *European Literature and the Latin Middle Ages*, p. 194.
38. Calkins, "Piero de' Crescenzi and the Medieval Garden," p. 172.
39. Ibid., p. 173.
40. Ibid., p. 164.
41. Harvey, *Mediaeval Gardens*, p. 10.
42. Ibid., pp. 92–93.
43. Hope, *Windsor Castle* 1, p. 70.
44. Ibid., p. 70.
45. Colvin, "Royal Gardens," p. 11.
46. Harvey, *Mediaeval Gardens*, p. 107.
47. Van Buren, "Reality and Literary Romance in the Park of Hesdin," pp. 120–22.

48. Murray and Addiss, "Plan and Space at Amiens Cathedral," pp. 50, 65.
49. De Certeau, *The Practice of Everyday Life*, p. 97.
50. Ibid., pp. 97–98.
51. From van Buren, "Reality and Literary Romance in the Park of Hesdin," figure 2.
52. Leslie, "An English Landscape Garden," p. 8.
53. Ibid., pp. 8–9.
54. Ibid., p. 14.
55. Colvin, "Royal Gardens," p. 20; see Harvey, *Mediaeval Gardens*, pp. 155–58, for list of paid gardeners.
56. Colvin, "Royal Gardens," p. 18; see also Doob, *The Idea of the Labyrinth*, pp. 106–7.
57. Colvin, "Royal Gardens," pp. 18–19.
58. Ibid., p. 20.
59. Harvey, *Mediaeval Gardens*, pp. 87–88. See also Underhill, "Elizabeth de Burgh," pp. 277–80, on her building ventures.
60. Thornton, *A History of Clare, Suffolk*, pp. 38–39.
61. Ibid., pp. 81–82.
62. Chaucer's employment in the household of the younger Elizabeth de Burgh began sometime in 1357, and he left the service of Prince Lionel sometime after October 1360, so he was not part of their household when they inherited Clare Castle the next year. See Crow and Olson, *Chaucer Life Records*, p. 20.
63. Goodman, *John of Gaunt*, p. 304.
64. Ibid., pp. 303, 305.
65. See Meyvaert, "The Medieval Monastic Garden," p. 44.
66. Harvey, *Mediaeval Gardens*, p. 85.
67. Ibid., p. 92.
68. Pearsall and Salter, *Landscapes and Seasons*, p. 74.
69. See Régnier-Bohler, "Imagining the Self," p. 322.
70. See, for example, Deschamps' *Le Lay de Franchise* and Machaut's *Le Jugement dou Roy de Behaingne*. See Kolve for an excellent discussion of how depictions of authors alone in gardens may indicate that authors conceived their material visually, and of how the act of *invenio* is depicted in manuscript illustrations (*Chaucer and the Imagery of Narrative*, pp. 32–42).

Chapter 2

1. Shoaf, "Notes Toward Chaucer's Poetics of Translation," p. 57; Leicester, "The Harmony of Chaucer's *Parlement*: A Dissonant Voice," p. 17.
2. Manley, "Chaucer and the Rhetoricians," pp. 274–75.
3. See Russell, *The English Dream Vision*, pp. 115–38, and Hanning, "Chaucer's First Ovid," pp. 121–63.

4. Kruger, *Dreaming in the Middle Ages*, pp. 134–35.

5. Muscatine, *Chaucer and the French Tradition*, p. 102. Similarly, Clemen discusses the poem's "love of the roundabout approach" (*Chaucer's Early Poetry*, p. 29), and Mehl examines Chaucer's "love of wide-ranging exposition and of seemingly aimless digression, and a deliberate delaying of the climax" (*Geoffrey Chaucer*, p. 28).

6. Several critics claim that such poems need to be understood in terms of spatial, rather than temporal, models. See Jordan, "The Compositional Structure"; Phillips, "Structure and Consolation"; and Walker, "Narrative Inconclusiveness and Consolatory Dialectic."

7. The importance of the garden as a transitional element is also argued by Jordan who writes that lines 344–443 serve "a compositional function as a transitional link between parts of the poetic structure" ("The Compositional Structure," p. 105), though the parts he refers to number eleven rather than two.

8. See Lawlor for a reading of this garden as an "Enchanted Garden" that "invokes the full power" of *amour courtois* ("The Pattern of Consolation," pp. 239, 256–58). Kiser ("Sleep, Dreams, and Poetry," p. 8) and Walker ("Narrative Inconclusiveness and Consolatory Dialectic, pp. 4–9) both claim that the *pleasance* or grove contrasts with Morpheus's cave in a relationship of positive to negative, life-affirming to life-denying, and even, in Walker's argument, divine or celestial bliss to dark hellishness. See also Fyler on the disjunction between the Golden Age, represented by the garden, and the intrusion of human consciousness in both the *Book of the Duchess* and the *Parliament of Fowls* (*Chaucer and Ovid*, pp. 65–95).

9. See, for example, Machaut's narrator in *Le Dit dou Lyon:* "Mais laissier vueil ceste matiere / Et revenir a la premiere, / N'orendroit plus n'en rimeray, / Pour ce qu'ailleurs a rimer ay" (*Oeuvres*, 2: 161, lines 67–70).

10. See Robertson, "The Book of the Duchess," pp. 332–40, for a good overview of the early criticism of the poem.

11. See Prior, "*Routhe* and *Hert-Huntyng*," pp. 10–11.

12. See especially Spearing on Chaucer's "associative structure" and on the relationship between Chaucer's dream-poems and Freud's theories of dreams (*Medieval Dream-Poetry*, pp. 49–73).

13. Gallo, *The Poetria Nova*, pp. 18–19.

14. Kelly notes that the distinction between natural and artistic narrative ordering was widely known and used by late medieval authors ("Theory of Composition in Medieval Narrative Poetry," p. 132). Harrison's early study concludes that all of the rhetorical figures used by Chaucer in the *Book of the Duchess* could be traced to his French models: "There was no need for [Chaucer] to open the textbooks" ("Medieval Rhetoric in the *Book of the Duchesse*," p. 442). Other critics have argued for Chaucer's application of Geoffrey's precepts. See especially Everett (*Essays on Middle English Literature*, p. 162) for a discussion of Chaucer's use of *amplificatio* and the seminal article by Manley, "Chaucer and the Rhetoricians."

15. Geoffrey of Vinsauf, *Poetria Nova*, p. 102.

16. While we do not know exactly when Chaucer read the *Poetria Nova* and there are only a few later references to the work (in *Troilus and Crisyede* I.1065–71 and the "Nun's Priest's Tale" VII.3347 ff.), it is quite probable that Chaucer was acquainted with Geoffrey's work and other *ars poetica* as he began his career as a narrative poet. On the influence of *Poetria Nova*, see M. C. Woods, *An Early Commentary*, pp. xvii–xviii.

17. Davis, *A Chaucer Glossary*, p. 150.

18. See Ferster, *Chaucer on Interpretation*, pp. 12–14, 69–93, and Hanning, "Chaucer and the Dangers of Poetry," pp. 18–20.

19. *Poetria Nova*, p. 90; trans. Gallo, p. 19.

20. Several critics have set the natural landscape of the garden against the conventional nature of the rest of the poem (for an example, see Burlin, *Chaucerian Fiction*, pp. 64–65). But I contend that the garden scene is itself as conventional as any other part of the poem and that its conventionality is one of its primary aspects.

21. Huppé and Robertson, *Fruyt and Chaf*, p. 55.

22. On shade, see Spearing, *Medieval Dream-Poetry*, pp. 17–18; Giamatti, *The Earthly Paradise*, p. 52; Curtius, *European Literature and the Latin Middle Ages*, pp. 195–200; and Stewart, *The Enclosed Garden*, pp. 60–96. For the opposite view, see Robertson, "Doctrine of Charity," p. 26.

23. Musa, trans., *The Divine Comedy*, p. 353.

24. Calkins, "Piero de' Crescenzi and the Medieval Garden," pp. 172–73.

25. Ibid., p. 172.

26. See also Calin, *The French Tradition*, pp. 276–89.

27. Lawton writes: "so much is plundered from the French tradition that hardly any structural or thematic element is unprecedented. Yet it *is* plundered, rather than borrowed, for it is wrenched quite ruthlessly from its original context" (*Chaucer's Narrators*, p. 52).

28. While scholars are not agreed on whether the extant Middle English translation of the *Roman* should be attributed to Chaucer, I would agree with Eckhardt for the A fragment's skill. It is also interesting to note that she discerns an "increase in the felt presence of the first-person narrator" ("The Art of Translation in *The Romaunt of the Rose*," p. 60), which echoes changes Chaucer makes to his sources in the *Book of the Duchess*.

29. Dahlberg, trans., *The Romance of the Rose*, p. 155.

30. See, for example, Coleman, *Medieval Readers and Writers: 1350–1400*, pp. 42–43, and Howard, *Chaucer: His Life, His Works, His World*, pp. 22–24.

31. See, for example, Spearing, *Medieval Dream-Poetry*, p. 72, and Hanning, "Chaucer's First Ovid," pp. 139–40.

32. See Spearing: "the introductory part ... serves to provide a psychological explanation for the dream that follows; and this is where Chaucer's originality as a dream-poet shows itself most strikingly" (*Medieval Dream-Poetry*, p. 55), and

Kiser: "*The Book of the Duchess* offers an early yet fully developed example of the complex Chaucerian persona" ("Sleep, Dreams, and Poetry," p. 3).

33. Gallo, *The Poetria Nova*, pp. 16–17.

34. Barney writes that "Chaucer often uses *proces* to mean nearly what we mean by plot or story: the word *discursive* in its etymology almost catches this sense" ("Suddenness and Process in Chaucer," p. 30). *Proces* may at times be related to *tale* in Chaucer's works, but the two do not necessarily imply one another.

35. See Kiser, "Sleep, Dreams, and Poetry," p. 4; Hanning, "Chaucer's First Ovid," p. 134; and Spearing, *Medieval Dream-Poetry*, p. 5.

36. For birdsong, see especially *Le Roman de la Rose*, lines 74–102, 631–90, and Machaut's *Le Dit dou Lyon*, lines 11–30; for other texts related to Guillaume de Lorris's *Roman*, see Windeatt's collection in *Sources* for a good selection; for the story of Troy, see Benoît de St. Maure, Guido de Columnis, and Joseph of Exeter; for examples of the hunt, see Marie de France's "Guigemar" and "Bisclavret" and Chrétien de Troyes' *Erec et Enide*.

37. Kiser, "Sleep, Dreams, and Poetry," p. 7.

38. A similar phenomenon is described by Leicester for the narrator of the *Parliament of Fowls*: "In trying to harmonize the materials of his dream with the traditional voices of his *auctores*, the poet constantly encounters the dissonance of those voices. He seems to wander among them, unable to make up his mind which to adopt, which part to speak, and the poem becomes a kind of late medieval and secular *sic et non* exacerbated" ("The Harmony of Chaucer's *Parlement*," pp. 20–21).

39. Nolan, "The Art of Expropriation," p. 206.

40. Mehl, *Geoffrey Chaucer*, p. 36.

41. Shoaf, "Stalking the Sorrowful H(e)art," p. 324.

42. Lynch, *The High Medieval Dream Vision*, p. 10.

43. See Edwards, "*The Book of the Duchess* and the Beginnings of Chaucer's Narrative"; Severs, "Chaucer's Self-Portrait in the *Book of the Duchess*"; Delany, *Naked Text*, p. 20; and Calin, *The French Tradition*, pp. 288–89.

44. For examples of readings that propose a resolution for the poem, see Frank, "Structure and Meaning in the *Parlement of Foules*," and Kelley, "Antithesis as the Principle of Design."

45. Leicester, "The Harmony of Chaucer's *Parlement*," p. 18.

46. See Heffernan, who argues that Chaucer "superimposes a garden of courtly love on one representation of productive love without creating easy reconciliations" ("Wells and Streams," p. 346), and McDonald, who finds that the garden description suggests "the sterility of the courtly conventions" ("An Interpretation," p. 283). Leicester acknowledges that "a conventional trope like the *locus amoenus* has, over the centuries, been subjected to a variety of particular treatments" ("The Harmony of Chaucer's *Parlement*," p. 18), but in his brief discussion of the Park of Paradise, he argues that "This vision [of the Park] stresses the clarity, harmony and order of the natural world by connecting it with the same

qualities in the supramundane realms" and that "the image stands in the poem as a brief fantasy of wish-fulfillment . . . which is quickly diffused" (p. 20).

47. On the extent of Chaucer's indebtedness to Dante on the gate's inscription, Schless notes the "similarity of their rhythm" (*Chaucer and Dante: A Revaluation*, p. 93), but he points out that inscriptions over gates are also found in the *Roman*, Boccaccio's *Amorosa visione*, and Froissart's "Le Cour de May" (p. 92). See Schildgen for a discussion of Dante's "Garden of God."

48. See also von Kreisler, "The *Locus Amoenus* and Eschatological Lore," who asserts a close translation from Boccaccio for this passage.

49. See Dante's *Purg.* XXVIII.1–42. J. A. W. Bennett also notes that Chaucer's narrator gains his paradise easily compared to Dante (*The Parlement of Foules: An Interpretation*, pp. 68–69). It may also be significant to Chaucer's reading of Dante that Dante falls asleep and has a dream in the canto preceding his entrance into the paradisal garden. Dante's passage also contains an allusion to Cytherea ("Citerea" XXVII.95).

50. Leicester notes that the passage is "an archetypal *poet's list*" that "calls attention to itself as a product of the speaker's act of recounting in the present" ("The Harmony of Chaucer's *Parlement*," pp. 21–22).

51. See, for instance, Froissart's *Le Paradys d'Amours*, lines 45ff.; Machaut's *Le Dit de la Fonteinne Amoureuse*, lines 1271ff.; and "Li Fablel dou Dieu d'Amors" lines 15ff.

52. See *Le Roman de la Rose*, lines 661ff.; compare *Book of the Duchess*, lines 307–8.

53. Davis et al. list this possible rendering only for this instance of the word (*A Chaucer Glossary*, p. 116).

54. Dahlberg, trans., *Roman de la Rose*, p. 337.

55. Both Leicester and Ferster have emphasized the importance of perception in this poem. In Leicester's words, during the first part of the poem the poet "subjects his *matere* to a kind of personal use which tends to make it expressive *merely* of his own subjectivity" ("The Harmony of Chaucer's *Parlement*," p. 22; emphasis original). Ferster claims that "in the *Parliament of Fowls* Chaucer gives a fuller picture of readers' actions upon texts in order to examine reading, and writing as a form of reading, as models for the mind's interaction with the world" ("Reading Nature," p. 189).

56. Musa, trans., *The Divine Comedy*, p. 352.

57. Frank, "Structure and Meaning in the *Parlement of Foules*," p. 537.

58. Lawton, *Chaucer's Narrators*, p. 42.

59. See Hanning on the liminal role of Machaut's fountain ("Chaucer's First Ovid," pp. 132–33) and Calin on the transformational role of the garden for Machaut's narrators (*A Poet at the Fountain*).

Chapter 3

1. See Salter, "*Troilus and Criseyde*: Poet and Narrator," pp. 281–91; Waswo, "The Narrator of *Troilus and Criseyde*"; and Delany's comments on the development of Chaucer's narrators in *The Naked Text*, pp. 29–34.

2. See Benton, "Clio and Venus," pp. 99–120, for a critique of the phrase "courtly love," but see Ferrante and Economou, *In Pursuit of Perfection*, pp. 3–9, for a defense of it in a literary context.

3. Muscatine, *Chaucer and the French Tradition*, pp. 129–32; Windeatt, "Chaucer and the *Filostrato*," p. 168; Taylor, *Chaucer Reads "The Divine Comedy*," p. 202. See also Wetherbee, *Chaucer and the Poets*, who argues that courtly values give way to spiritual insight in the poem. Windeatt's *Oxford Guides to Chaucer:* Troilus and Criseyde is an invaluable guide to much of the criticism of this poem.

4. Lewis, "What Chaucer Really Did to *Il Filostrato*"; Payne, *The Key of Remembrance*, pp. 177–88; Wallace, *Chaucer and the Early Writings of Boccaccio*, pp. 106–40; Windeatt, "Chaucer and the *Filostrato*," pp. 170–78.

5. For a discussion of Chaucer's process of "in-eching," see Windeatt's introduction to his edition of *Troilus and Criseyde*, pp. 7–11. See Smyser, "The Domestic Background," for an analysis of architectural spaces.

6. For a complete list of lyric passages in *Troilus and Criseyde*, see Wimsatt, "The French Element in *Troilus and Criseyde*." For an interpretation based on the poem's "lyric cores," see Vance, *Mervelous Signals*, p. 271.

7. R. K. Gordon, trans., *The Story of Troilus*, pp. 67–69.

8. Ibid., p. 61.

9. Ibid., pp. 72–73.

10. Again I use Jauss's phrase (*Toward an Aesthetic of Reception*, p. 88). See Windeatt's discussion of other ways in which Chaucer enhances the generic romance elements in the poem in "'Troilus' and the Disenchantment of Romance."

11. See Smyser, "The Domestic Background," p. 304.

12. In the *Filostrato*, it is clear that Pandarus makes the scene up out of whole cloth. Further, Boccaccio has the scene take place in a forest, not a garden.

13. Muscatine, *Chaucer and the French Tradition*, p. 137; Windeatt, "'Troilus' and the Disenchantment of Romance," p. 131.

14. See Fyler, "The Fabrications of Pandarus," for a discussion of other instances of Pandarus's invention.

15. See especially II.421ff. It seems possible that Criseyde might have preferred a second marriage to an affair, and her uncle, as her only male relative in Troy, would have served as her surrogate father in arranging a second marriage for her. But see Hallissy, *Clean Maids, True Wives, Steadfast Widows*, pp. 150–51, for a very different view.

16. See Duby on situations that often faced widows of the upper classes, particularly those without children (*The Knight, the Lady and the Priest*, pp. 128, 143). Aers attributes Criseyde's reluctance to her knowledge that the courtly love system requires her to relinquish her subjectivity (*Community, Gender, and Individual Identity*, pp. 130–38).

17. See Wimsatt, "Guillaume de Machaut and Chaucer's *Troilus and Criseyde.*"

18. Sister Borthwick ("Antigone's Song as 'Mirour'") and I. Gordon (*The Double Sorrow of Troilus*, p. 98) argue that Antigone's song answers Criseyde's fears. On the song as an example of Criseyde's "self-interested interpretation," see Kiser, *Truth and Textuality in Chaucer's Poetry*, pp. 67–68.

19. Sister Borthwick also finds this "dark side" of love in Antigone's song, though her conclusions differ markedly from mine ("Antigone's Song as 'Mirour,'" pp. 227–28).

20. Many scholars have written on this passage. See, for example, Wetherbee, *Chaucer and the Poets*, pp. 187–88; Nolan, *Chaucer and the Tradition of the Roman Antique*, pp. 240–42; Fries, "(Almost) Without a Song"; and Kinney, "'Who made this song?'"

21. Baswell and Taylor, "The Faire Queene Eleyne in Chaucer's *Troilus*," pp. 293–311.

22. R. K. Gordon, trans., *The Story of Troilus*, p. 67.

23. Ibid., p. 67.

24. While many critics have outlined the similarities between Helen and Criseyde, others have pointed out their differences. McAlpine, for example, argues forcefully that Criseyde struggles to avoid Helen's fate in this poem (*The Genre of* Troilus and Crisyede, pp. 189–90).

25. See Dodd, who claims that "The courtly love doctrine most prominent in the *Troilus* is perhaps the doctrine of secrecy" (*Courtly Love in Chaucer and Gower*, p. 135), and Windeatt: "Chaucer consistently draws a society that allows much less privacy to his lovers, while at the same time he gives to his characters a much increased sense that their love affair must be secret" ("'Love That Oughte Ben Secree'," p. 116), and his further comments in "'Troilus' and the Disenchantment of Romance," p. 146.

26. Walsh, *Andreas Capellanus on Love*, pp. 282–83.

27. Benson, ed., *The Riverside Chaucer*, p. 420.

28. Ibid., pp. 420–21.

29. Ferrante, "The Conflict of Lyric Conventions and Romance Form," p. 144.

30. Ibid., p. 173.

31. Ferrante's discussion distinguishes variations on the theme of courtly love versus society in all of these works and so is more involved than my summary would indicate. See also Diamond on the conflict between medieval hierarchical society and the ideal of love and harmony between the sexes ("*Troilus and Crisyede:* The Politics of Love," pp. 93–103).

32. See Taylor, "*Inferno* 5 and *Troilus and Criseyde* Revisited," p. 246, on Criseyde and the conventional roles of romance.

33. See also Taylor, "*Inferno* 5 and *Troilus and Criseyde* Revisited," pp. 252–54, and Aers (*Community, Gender, and Individual Identity*, pp. 130–31) for discussions of Criseyde's conflicting images of herself.

34. See Hanning, "Come in Out of the Code," pp. 120–37, for a discussion of the very different ways in which the two authors represent desire.

Chapter 4

1. Martin, *Chaucer's Women*, p. 111. Her chapter "Real Women in Imaginary Gardens" arrives at some of the same conclusions as I do here, but her analysis does not detail changes Chaucer made to his sources for garden descriptions.

2. Power, *Medieval Women*, p. 38.

3. McNamara and Wemple, "The Power of Women Through the Family."

4. Judith Bennett, "Public Power and Authority," p. 21.

5. See Power, *Medieval Women*, p. 40, and Duby, *The Knight, the Lady and the Priest*, pp. 171–72.

6. On changes to marital financial arrangements, see Duby, *The Knight, the Lady and the Priest*, pp. 97–104; on the financial status of widows, see pp. 128, 143.

7. My work on Chaucer's female characters has been greatly influenced by that of Hanning, particularly his article "From *Eva* and *Ave* to Eglentyne and Alisoun," and Ferrante, regarding medieval representations of women (*Woman as Image in Medieval Literature*).

8. Other Chaucerians who have applied Bakhtin's literary theory to the works of Chaucer include Ganim, *Chaucerian Theatricality*, and Knapp, *Chaucer and the Social Contest*. See also the exchange between Engle and McClellan in *Exemplaria* 1.2 (1989). But no one to my knowledge has analyzed the author/narrator split in Chaucer's discourse in light of Bakhtin's theory of dialogic discourse.

9. Ganim asserts that novelistic discourse exists when "the authority of a single dominant dialect of language breaks down.... The art of the novel is to let voices other than those of the author speak" ("Bakhtin, Chaucer, Carnival, Lent," p. 62). In this sense, Chaucer's works qualify as "novelistic."

10. Bakhtin, *The Dialogic Imagination*, p. 46.

11. Critics who tend to blame Criseyde for leaving Troy, often at the same time that they acknowledge that she was traded to the Greeks, include Burnley, "Criseyde's Heart and the Weakness of Women," and Lambert, "*Troilus*, Books I–III: A Criseydan Reading."

12. Diamond has argued for the essential conservatism of Chaucer's work, claiming that he can only mouth the prevailing antifeminism of his time

("Chaucer's Women and Women's Chaucer"). See also Hansen's provocative article, which concludes that a feminist reading of the *Tales* reveals "structures of antifeminism" and "displacement and usurpation of female silence" ("The Wife of Bath and the Mark of Adam," p. 414) and her far more detailed study of the issue, *Chaucer and the Fictions of Gender.*

13. While Kolve argues that Emelye seems free at first, since she can enter and leave her garden at will, he goes on to point out that the privileged life the garden represents becomes a prison as surely as the prison tower and the prison of love do: "the literal prison where the knights fall in love expands into a metaphoric prison that includes all human life" (*Chaucer and the Imagery of Narrative*, p. 98). See also Hanning, "'The Struggle between Noble Designs and Chaos'," especially pp. 537–38.

14. Donaldson writes of Emelye: "She has no mind or character of her own, desiring only what most desires her" (*Speaking of Chaucer*, p. 50). William Woods argues that she "lack[s] almost every individualizing feature" ("Chivalry and Nature in *The Knight's Tale*," p. 295). Critics also take the Knight's characterization of her as a flower at face value. See, for example, Stock, "The Two Mayings," p. 209.

15. Crane, *Gender and Romance*, p. 170.

16. Stock suggests that the green dress Emelye wears on her hunting party expedition "mimics not Diana but Venus" ("The Two Mayings," p. 211), placing her in a more ambiguous context than Boccaccio provides for his Emilia. See Crane for a discussion of Emelye's "lethal beauty" (*Gender and Romance*, p. 81).

17. See also Crane on the Amazons and Theban widows (*Gender and Romance*, pp. 18–23). See Hanning on the violent images and acts that punctuate the tale ("'The Struggle between Noble Designs and Chaos'," pp. 534–38) and Kempton, "Chaucer's Knight and the Knight's Theseus," pp. 238–243. Howard discusses especially well the chivalric ideal articulated in the tale (*The Idea of the* Canterbury Tales, pp. 227–37).

18. See Kolve, *Chaucer and the Imagery of Narrative*, pp. 87–157, for a detailed discussion of several illuminations from the same manuscript.

19. Crane, *Gender and Romance*, p. 174.

20. Stock compares the two scenes but concludes that Arcite's Maying serves to distinguish him from Palamon, rather than finding, as I do, a vast difference between the activities allowed him and Emelye ("The Two Mayings").

21. Several critics claim instead that Emelye desires to marry. Stock, for example, writes that Palamon, Arcite, *and Emelye* "are granted what they request" from the deities ("The Two Mayings," p. 220). Howard also seems to assume that Emelye is accommodating rather than entrapped: "a good medieval lady, [Emelye] wishes first chastity, and, failing that, whoever desires her most" (*The Idea of the* Canterbury Tales, p. 236). Martin, however, notes how Emelye's "vision of freedom" contradicts the opportunities offered her (*Chaucer's Women*, p. 107), and Crane identifies Emelye's "resistance" as the adventure of the tale (*Gender and Romance*, p. 174).

22. *Queynte*, possibly a modified form of ME *cunte* from ON *kunta* (Davis, *A Chaucer Glossary*, p. 115), as a name for female genitalia, is attested in Chaucer's *Miller's Tale* (I.3276) and the *Wyf of Bath's Prologue* (III.332, 444). See Crane, *Gender and Romance*, pp. 177–78.

23. See Bryan and Dempster, eds., *Sources and Analogues of Chaucer's* Canterbury Tales, pp. 333–40.

24. On the figure of Priapus, see Brown, "*Hortus Inconclusus*," and Hoffman, "Ovid's Priapus in the *Merchant's Tale*." On wells in the tale, see Heffernan, "Wells and Streams," pp. 348–49.

25. Chaucer translates the passage: "Ne grew there tree in mannes syghte / So fayr, ne so wel woxe in highte" (*Romaunt* 1459–60).

26. See lines 139–462 in the *Roman* for the full description. Of course, these figures may indicate that, because of the sinful nature of Déduit's garden, any entrant into the garden will experience old age, hatred, poverty, and so on. The ambiguity, I believe, marks well the difference between Guillaume de Lorris's garden and the garden redefined by Jean de Meun.

27. See Calin, *The French Tradition*, p. 322, for a reading of Machaut's influence on January's garden.

28. Aers argues that May is essentially purchased by January and that she is treated as a commodity (*Chaucer, Langland and the Creative Imagination*, pp. 152–54).

29. On the parallels with Pluto and Proserpine, see Wetherbee, *Chaucer: The Canterbury Tales*, p. 73; Donovon, "The Image of Pluto and Proserpine in the *Merchant's Tale*"; and Pratt, "Chaucer's Claudian."

30. See the Sermons on the Song of Songs written by St. Bernard of Clairvaux for warnings against such interpretations, especially Sermon 1, section 12 (Leclercq, ed., *Sancti Bernardi Opera*).

31. In the Wife of Bath's words, "He seith that to be wedded is no synne; / Bet is to be wedded than to brynne" (III.51–52). See also Kee, "Two Chaucerian Gardens," p. 159–61; Robertson, "The Doctrine of Charity," pp. 45–46; and Kellogg's article on the association of Susannah's garden with January's garden ("Susannah and the 'Merchant's Tale'"). For a discussion of the Song of Songs in the 'Miller's Tale,' see Kaske, "The *Canticum Canticorum*."

32. Bleeth argues that January's laurel tree recalls Joseph's flowering rod, establishing an analogy between the two husbands as well as their wives, May and Mary. But Bleeth goes on to argue that May resembles Eve more closely than she does Mary ("The Image of Paradise in the *Merchant's Tale*," especially pp. 64–65).

33. On the fabliau as a genre that is defined by the transgression of boundaries, including gender, see Benkov, "Language and Women: From Silence to Speech," and Allen, "The Ambiguity of Silence."

34. See Ganim ("Carnival Voices") for an excellent discussion of how exemplary narratives may have the opposite effect from that desired by their narrators.

35. Kittredge argued that the *Franklin's Tale* provided the resolution to the implied question of what makes a good marriage ("Chaucer's Discussion of Marriage"). After years of dissent among Chaucerians from this view, several critics have come to agree with Kittredge's formulation, among them Fyler ("Love and Degree in the *Franklin's Tale*") and Jacobs ("The Marriage Contract of the *Franklin's Tale:* The Remaking of Society").

36. In Boccaccio's *Filocolo,* one of Chaucer's sources for this tale, a garden is the *locus* for the *questioni d'amore.* Ferster notes that "Dorigen's playful response to Aurelius is influenced by the context provided by the garden: gardens are places to play in" ("Interpretation and Imitation in Chaucer's *Franklin's Tale,*" p. 163). See also Kee, "Two Chaucerian Gardens," pp. 161–62, and Heffernan, "Wells and Streams," p. 350. Both assert that the use of the garden in the *Franklin's Tale* reinforces the ideal of Arveragus and Dorigen's marriage.

37. Critics invariably note the importance of magic and metamorphosis to this tale, but there appears to be no discussion among scholars regarding the metamorphosis of Dorigen's playful promise.

38. Walsh, *Andreas Capellanus on Love,* pp. 72–73.

39. Ibid.

40. Ibid.

41. Vance, *Mervelous Signals,* p. 281.

42. See especially Shoaf, who claims that Dorigen is a victim of her own superficial reading of events and compares her to the figure of Medusa ("The *Franklin's Tale:* Chaucer and Medusa").

43. See Duby on the practice of repudiating adulterous wives as a way of ending a marriage (*The Knight, the Lady and the Priest,* p. 175).

44. For example, Rudat argues that the magician is the most generous person in the tale in "Gentillesse and the Marriage Debate in the *Franklin's Tale,*" and Magnus claims that Arveragus holds to the "highest level of consciousness" when he insists Dorigen sleep with Aurelius ("The Hem of Philosophy," p. 15).

45. Martin, *Chaucer's Women,* p. 130. But Martin does not make the further observation that Dorigen, having played by the rules of courtly banter, finds herself trapped by them. Instead, Martin, like scores of other Chaucerians, labels Dorigen's playful promise "foolish" (p. 122) and "rash" (p. 123).

Bibliography

Aers, David. *Chaucer, Langland and the Creative Imagination.* London: Routledge and Kegan Paul, 1980.
———. *Community, Gender, and Individual Identity: English Writing 1360–1430.* London: Routledge, 1988.
Allen, Peter L. "The Ambiguity of Silence: Gender, Writing, and *Le Roman de Silence.*" In *Sign, Sentence, Discourse: Language in Medieval Thought and Literature,* ed. Julian Wasserman and Lois Roney, 98–112. Syracuse: Syracuse University Press, 1989.
Andreas Capellanus. See Walsh.
Appleton, Jay. *The Experience of Landscape.* London: Wiley, 1975.
Bachelard, Gaston. *The Poetics of Space,* trans. Maria Jolas. Boston: Beacon Press, 1964.
Bakhtin, Mikhail. *The Dialogic Imagination,* ed. Michael Holquist, trans. Caryl Emerson and M. Holquist. Austin: University of Texas Press, 1981.
Barney, Stephen A. "Suddenness and Process in Chaucer." *Chaucer Review* 16 (1981): 18–37.
Baswell, Christopher, and P. B. Taylor. "The Faire Queene Eleyne in Chaucer's *Troilus.*" *Speculum* 63 (1988): 293–311.
Baumgartner, Emmanuèle. "The Play of Temporalities; or, The Reported Dream of Guillaume de Lorris." In *Rethinking the* Romance of the Rose: *Text, Image, Reception,* ed. Kevin Bronlee and Sylvia Huot, 22–38. Philadelphia: University of Pennsylvania Press, 1992.
Benkov, Edith Joyce. "Language and Women: From Silence to Speech." In *Sign, Sentence, Discourse: Language in Medieval Thought and Literature,* ed. Julian Wasserman and Lois Roney, 245–65. Syracuse: Syracuse University Press, 1989.
Bennett, J. A. W. *The Parlement of Foules: An Interpretation.* Oxford: Clarendon Press, 1957.
Bennett, Judith M. "Public Power and Authority in the Medieval English Coun-

tryside." In *Women and Power in the Middle Ages*, ed. Mary Erler and Maryanne Kowaleski, 18–36. Athens: University of Georgia Press, 1988.

Benoît de Sainte-Maure. *Le Roman de Troie*, ed. Leopold Constans. Société des Anciens Textes Français 50. Paris: Firmin-Didot, 1904–12.

Benson, Larry D., ed. *The Riverside Chaucer.* 3d ed. Boston: Houghton Mifflin Co., 1987.

Benton, John F. "Clio and Venus: A Historical View of Medieval Love." In *Culture, Power and Personality in Medieval France*, ed. Thomas N. Bisson, 99–120. London: Hambledon Press, 1991. Rpt. from *The Meaning of Courtly Love*, ed. F. X. Newman, 19–42. Albany: State University of New York Press, 1968.

Bernard of Clairvaux. *Sancti Bernardi Opera*, ed. J. Leclercq et al. Rome: Editiones Cistercienses, 1957. Trans. Irene Edwards as *On the Song of Songs*. Kalamazoo, Mich.: Cistercian Publications, 1980.

Biblia sacra iuxta vulgata versionem. 2d ed. Ed. Robert Weber. Stuttgart: Württembergische Bibelanstalt, 1975.

Bleeth, Kenneth A. "The Image of Paradise in the *Merchant's Tale*." In *The Learned and the Lewd: Studies in Honor of Bartlett Jere Whiting*, ed. Larry D. Benson, 45–60. Cambridge: Harvard University Press, 1974.

Boccaccio, Giovanni. *Opere Minori in Volgare*, vol. 2, ed. Mario Marti. Milan: Rizzoli, 1970.

Boitani, Piero, ed. *Chaucer and the Italian Trecento.* Cambridge: Cambridge University Press, 1983.

Borthwick, Mary Charlotte. "Antigone's Song as 'Mirour' in Chaucer's *Troilus and Criseyde*." *Modern Language Quarterly* 22 (1961): 227–35.

Brown, Emerson L., Jr. "*Hortus Inconclusus:* The Significance of Priapus and Pyramus and Thisbe in the *Merchant's Tale*." *Chaucer Review* 4 (1970): 31–40.

Brownlee, Kevin, and Sylvia Huot, eds. *Rethinking the* Romance of the Rose: *Text, Image, Reception*. Philadelphia: University of Pennsylvania Press, 1992.

Bryan, W. F., and Germaine Dempster, eds. *Sources and Analogues of Chaucer's Canterbury Tales*. Atlantic Highlands, N.J.: Humanities Press, 1958.

Burlin, Robert M. *Chaucerian Fiction.* Princeton: Princeton University Press, 1977.

Burnley, J. D. "Criseyde's Heart and the Weakness of Women: An Essay in Lexical Interpretation." *Studia Neophilologica* 54 (1982): 25–38.

Burrow, J. A., ed. *Geoffrey Chaucer: A Critical Anthology.* Baltimore: Penguin, 1969.

Calin, William. *The French Tradition and the Literature of Medieval England.* Toronto: University of Toronto Press, 1994.

———. *A Poet at the Fountain: Essays on the Narrative Verse of Guillaume de Machaut.* Lexington: University of Kentucky Press, 1974.

Calkins, Robert G. "Piero de' Crescenzi and the Medieval Garden." In *Medieval Gardens*, ed. Elisabeth B. MacDougall, 157–73. Washington, D.C.: Dumbarton Oaks, 1986.

Carruthers, Mary. *The Book of Memory: A Study of Memory in Medieval Culture.* Cambridge: Cambridge University Press, 1990.

———. "The Poet as Master Builder: Composition and Locational Memory in the Middle Ages." *New Literary History* 24 (1993): 881–904.

Chaucer, Geoffrey. *The Riverside Chaucer.* 3d ed. Ed. Larry D. Benson. Boston: Houghton Mifflin Co., 1987.

———. *Troilus and Criseyde,* ed. B. A. Windeatt. New York: Longman, 1984.

Chrétien de Troyes. *Erec et Enide,* ed. Mario Rogues. Paris: Champion, 1952.

[Cicero]. *Ad C. Herennium: Dei Ratione Dicendi (Rhetorica ad Herennium),* trans. Harry Caplan. Cambridge: Harvard University Press, 1954.

Claudian. *De raptu Proserpinae,* ed. J. B. Hall. Cambridge: Cambridge University Press, 1969. In *Claudian,* trans. Maurice Platnauer as "The Rape of Proserpine," 293–377. Cambridge: Harvard University Press, 1922; rpt. 1956.

———. "Epithalamium de nuptiis Honorii Augusti." In *Claudian,* vol. 1, ed. and trans. Maurice Platnauer, 240–67. Cambridge: Harvard University Press, 1956.

Clemen, Wolfgang. *Chaucer's Early Poetry,* trans. C. A. M. Sym. London: Methuen and Company, 1963.

Coleman, Janet. *Medieval Readers and Writers: 1350–1400.* New York: Columbia University Press, 1981.

Colvin, Howard M. "Royal Gardens in Medieval England." In *Medieval Gardens,* ed. Elisabeth MacDougall, 9–22. Washington, D.C.: Dum-barton Oaks, 1986.

Comito, Terry. *The Idea of the Garden in the Renaissance.* New Brunswick, N.J.: Rutgers University Press, 1978.

Cosgrove, Denis. *Social Formation and Symbolic Landscape.* London: Croom Helm, 1984.

Crane, Susan. *Gender and Romance in Chaucer's* Canterbury Tales. Princeton: Princeton University Press, 1994.

Crow, Martin M., and Clair C. Olson. *Chaucer Life Records.* Oxford: Clarendon Press, 1966.

Curtius, Ernst Robert. *European Literature and the Latin Middle Ages,* trans. Willard R. Trask. Bollingen Series 36. Princeton: Princeton University Press, 1953.

Dahlberg, Charles, trans. *The Romance of the Rose.* Hanover, N.H.: University Press of New England, 1983.

Daley, Brian E. "The 'Closed Garden' and the 'Sealed Fountain': Song of Songs 4:12 in the Late Medieval Iconography of Mary." In *Medieval Gardens,* ed. Elisabeth B. MacDougall, 255–78. Washington, D.C.: Dumbarton Oaks, 1986.

Dante Alighieri. *La Commedia secondo l'antica vulgata,* ed. Giorgio Petrocchi. Torino: Giulio Einaudi, 1975. Trans. Mark Musa as "The Divine Comedy" in *The Portable Dante,* 3–585. New York: Penguin, 1995.

Davis, Norman, et al. *A Chaucer Glossary.* Oxford: Clarendon Press, 1979.

de Certeau, Michel. *The Practice of Everyday Life,* trans. Steven F. Rendall. Berkeley: University of California Press, 1984.

Delany, Sheila. *The Naked Text: Chaucer's* Legend of Good Women. Berkeley: University of California Press, 1994.
Deschamps, Eustache. *Oeuvres Complètes,* ed. Le Marquis de Queux de Saint-Hilaire. Société des Anciens Textes Français 9. Paris: Firmin-Didot, 1878–1903. "Ballade addressed to Chaucer," ed. and trans. J. A. Burrow. In *Geoffrey Chaucer: A Critical Anthology,* 26–28. Baltimore: Penguin, 1969.
Diamond, Arlyn. "Chaucer's Women and Women's Chaucer." In *The Authority of Experience: Essays in Feminist Criticism,* ed. A. Diamond and Lee R. Edwards, 60–83. Amherst: University of Massachusetts Press, 1977.
———. *"Troilus and Criseyde:* The Politics of Love." In *Chaucer in the Eighties,* ed. Julian N. Wasserman and Robert J. Blanch, 93–103. Syracuse: Syracuse University Press, 1986.
Dinshaw, Carolyn. *Chaucer's Sexual Poetics.* Madison: University of Wisconsin Press, 1989.
Dodd, William George. *Courtly Love in Chaucer and Gower.* Harvard Studies in English, vol. 1. Gloucester, Mass.: Peter Smith, 1959.
Donaldson, E. Talbot. *Speaking of Chaucer.* New York: Norton, 1970.
Donovon, Mortimer J. "The Image of Pluto and Proserpine in the *Merchant's Tale." Philological Quarterly* 36 (1957): 49–60.
Doob, Penelope Reed. *The Idea of the Labyrinth from Classical Antiquity Through the Middle Ages.* Ithaca: Cornell University Press, 1990.
Duby, Georges. *The Knight, the Lady and the Priest: The Making of Modern Marriage in Medieval France,* trans. Barbara Bray. New York: Pantheon, 1983.
Eckhardt, Caroline D. "The Art of Translation in *The Romaunt of the Rose." Studies in the Age of Chaucer* 6 (1984): 41–63.
Edwards, Robert. *"The Book of the Duchess* and the Beginnings of Chaucer's Narrative." *New Literary History* 13 (1982): 189–204.
———. *The Dream of Chaucer: Representation and Reflection in the Early Narratives.* Durham: Duke University Press, 1989.
Engle, Lars. "Chaucer, Bakhtin, and Griselda." *Exemplaria* 1.2 (1989): 429–460.
Everett, Dorothy. *Essays on Middle English Literature,* ed. Patricia Kean. London: Oxford University Press, 1955.
Ferrante, Joan M. "The Conflict of Lyric Conventions and Romance Form." In *In Pursuit of Perfection: Courtly Love in Medieval Literature,* ed. Joan M. Ferrante and George D. Economou, 135–78. Port Washington, N.Y.: Kennikat Press, 1975.
———. *Woman as Image in Medieval Literature: From the Twelfth Century to Dante.* New York: Columbia University Press, 1975.
Ferrante, Joan M., and George D. Economou, eds. *In Pursuit of Perfection: Courtly Love in Medieval Literature.* Port Washington, N.Y.: Kennikat Press, 1975.
Ferster, Judith. *Chaucer on Interpretation.* Cambridge: Cambridge University Press, 1984.

———. "Interpretation and Imitation in Chaucer's *Franklin's Tale.*" In *Medieval Literature: Criticism, Ideology, and History,* ed. David Aers, 148–68. New York: St. Martin's Press, 1986.

———. "Reading Nature: the Phenomenology of Reading in the *Parliament of Fowls. Mediaevalia* 3 (1977): 189–213.

Frank, Robert Worth, Jr. "Structure and Meaning in the *Parlement of Foules.*" *PMLA* 71 (1956): 530–39.

Fries, Maureen. "(Almost) Without a Song: Criseyde and Lyric in Chaucer's *Troilus.*" *Chaucer Yearbook* 1 (1992): 47–63.

Froissart, Jean. *Oeuvres: Poésies,* ed. M. Aug. Scheler. Brussels: Victor Devaux et Cie., 1870–71.

Fyler, John M. *Chaucer and Ovid.* New Haven: Yale University Press, 1979.

———. "The Fabrications of Pandarus." *Modern Language Quarterly* 41 (1980): 115–30. Rpt. in *Chaucer's* Troilus and Criseyde: *"Subgit Be to Alle Poesye,"* ed. R. A. Shoaf, 107–19. Binghamton, N.Y.: Medieval and Renaissance Texts and Studies, 1992.

———. "Love and Degree in the *Franklin's Tale.*" *Chaucer Review* 21 (1987): 321–37.

Gallo, Ernest. *The Poetria Nova and Its Sources in Early Rhetorical Doctrine.* The Hague: Mouton, 1971.

Ganim, John M. "Bakhtin, Chaucer, Carnival, Lent." *Studies in the Age of Chaucer, Proceedings* 2 (1986): 59–71.

———."Carnival Voices and the Envoy to the *Clerk's Tale.*" *Chaucer Review* 22 (1987): 112–27.

———. *Chaucerian Theatricality.* Princeton: Princeton University Press, 1990.

———. *Style and Consciousness in Middle English Narrative.* Princeton: Princeton University Press, 1983.

Geoffrey of Vinsauf. "Poetria Nova." In *Les Arts Poétiques du XIIe et du XIIIe Siècle,* ed. Edmond Faral, 194–262. Paris: Champion, 1958.

Giamatti, A. Bartlett. *The Earthly Paradise and the Renaissance Epic.* Princeton: Princeton University Press, 1966.

Goodman, Anthony. *John of Gaunt: The Exercise of Princely Power in Fourteenth-Century Europe.* Hawlow, England: Longman, 1992.

Gordon, Ida. *The Double Sorrow of Troilus: A Study of Ambiguities in* Troilus and Criseyde. Oxford: Clarendon Press, 1970.

Gordon, R. K., trans. "Filostrato." In *The Story of Troilus.* Medieval Academy Reprints for Teaching #2, 25–127. Toronto: University of Toronto Press, 1978.

Guido de Columnis. *Historia Destructionis Troiae,* ed. Nathaniel E. Griffin. Cambridge, Mass.: Mediaeval Academy, 1936.

Guillaume de Lorris and Jean de Meun. *Le Roman de la Rose,* ed. Ernest Langlois. Société des Anciens Textes Français 62. Paris: Firmin-Didot, Champion, 1914–24. Trans. Charles Dahlberg as *The Romance of the Rose.* Hanover, N.H.: University Press of New England, 1983.

Guillaume de Machaut. *Oeuvres,* ed. Ernest Hoepffner. Société des Anciens Textes Français 56. Paris: Firmin-Didot, 1908–1921.

Hallissy, Margaret. *Clean Maids, True Wives, Steadfast Widows: Chaucer's Women and Medieval Codes of Conduct.* Westport, Conn.: Greenwood Press, 1993.

Hanning, Robert W. "Chaucer and the Dangers of Poetry." *The CEA Critic* 46 (1984): 17–26.

———. "Chaucer's First Ovid: Metamorphosis and Poetic Tradition in *The Book of the Duchess* and *The House of Fame.*" In *Chaucer and the Craft of Fiction,* ed. Leigh A. Arrathoon, 121–63. Rochester, Minn.: Solaris Press, 1986.

———. "Come in Out of the Code: Interpreting the Discourse of Desire in Boccaccio's *Filostrato* and Chaucer's *Troilus and Criseyde.*" In *Chaucer's* Troilus and Criseyde: *"Subgit Be to Alle Poesye,"* ed. R. A. Shoaf, 120–37. Binghamton, N.Y.: Medieval and Renaissance Texts and Studies, 1992.

———. "From *Eva* and *Ave* to Eglentyne and Alisoun: Chaucer's Insight into the Roles Women Play." *Signs* 2 (1977): 580–99.

———. "'The Struggle between Noble Designs and Chaos': The Literary Tradition of Chaucer's *Knight's Tale.*" *The Literary Review* 23 (1980): 519–41.

Hansen, Elaine Tuttle. *Chaucer and the Fictions of Gender.* Berkeley: University of California Press, 1992.

———. "The Wife of Bath and the Mark of Adam." *Women's Studies* 15.4 (1988): 399–416.

Harrison, Benjamin S. "Medieval Rhetoric in the *Book of the Duchesse.*" *PMLA* 49 (1934): 428–42.

Harvey, John H. *Mediaeval Gardens.* Beaverton, Ore.: Timber Press, 1981.

Heffernan, Carol Falvo. "Wells and Streams in Three of Chaucer's Gardens." *Papers on Language and Literature* 15 (1979): 339–57.

Hoffman, Richard. "Ovid's Priapus in the *Merchant's Tale.*" *ELN* 111 (1965–66): 169–72.

Hope, W. H. St. J. *Windsor Castle: An Architectural History.* London: Office of Country Life, 1913.

Howard, Donald R. *Chaucer: His Life, His Works, His World.* New York: E. P. Dutton, 1987.

———. *The Idea of the* Canterbury Tales. Berkeley: University of California Press, 1976.

Howes, Laura L. "Cultured Nature in Chaucer's Early Dream Poems." In *The Medieval World of Nature,* ed. Joyce E. Salisbury, 187–200. New York: Garland Press, 1993.

Hult, David F. "Language and Dismemberment: Abelard, Origen, and the *Romance of the Rose.*" In *Rethinking the* Romance of the Rose: *Text, Image, Reception,* ed. Kevin Brownlee and Sylvia Huot, 101–30. Philadelphia: University of Pennsylvania Press, 1992.

Huppé, Bernard F., and D. W. Robertson, Jr. *Fruyt and Chaf: Studies in Chaucer's Allegories*. Princeton: Princeton University Press, 1963.

Jacobs, Kathryn. "The Marriage Contract of the *Franklin's Tale:* The Remaking of Society." *Chaucer Review* 20 (1986): 132–143.

Jauss, Hans Robert. *Toward an Aesthetic of Reception,* trans. Timothy Bahti. Theory and History of Literature, vol. 2. Minneapolis: University of Minnesota Press, 1982.

Jean de Meun. *Le Roman de la Rose*. See Guillaume de Lorris.

Jellicoe, Sir Geoffrey, et al., eds. *The Oxford Companion to Gardens*. Oxford: Oxford University Press, 1986.

Jordan, Robert M. "The Compositional Structure of the *Book of the Duchess. Chaucer Review* 9 (1974): 99–117.

Joseph of Exeter. *Werke und Brief,* ed. Ludwig Gompf. Leiden: E. J. Brill, 1970. *Trojan War I-III,* trans. A. K. Bate. Wiltshire, England: Aris and Phillips, 1986.

Kaske, R. E. "The *Canticum Canticorum* and the *Miller's Tale.*" *Studies in Philology* 59 (1962): 479–500.

Kee, Kenneth. "Two Chaucerian Gardens." *Medieval Studies* 23 (1961): 154–62.

Kelley, Michael R. "Antithesis as the Principle of Design in the *Parlement of Foules.*" *Chaucer Review* 14 (1979): 61–73.

Kellogg, Alfred L. "Susannah and the 'Merchant's Tale'." *Speculum* 35 (1960): 275–79.

Kelly, Douglas. "Theory of Composition in Medieval Narrative Poetry and Geoffrey of Vinsauf's *Poetria Nova.*" *Medieval Studies* 31 (1969): 117–48.

Kempton, Daniel. "Chaucer's Knight and the Knight's Theseus: 'And Though That He Was Worthy, He Was Wise.'" *Journal of Narrative Technique* 17 (1987): 237–58.

Kinney, Clare Regan. "'Who Made This Song?': The Engendering of Lyric Counterplots in *Troilus and Criseyde.*" *Studies in Philology* 89 (1992): 272–92.

Kiser, Lisa J. "Sleep, Dreams, and Poetry in Chaucer's *Book of the Duchess.*" *Papers on Language and Literature* 19 (1983): 3–12.

———. *Truth and Textuality in Chaucer's Poetry*. Hanover: University Press of New England, 1991.

Kittredge, George Lyman. "Chaucer's Discussion of Marriage." *Modern Philology* 9 (1912): 435–67.

Knapp, Peggy. *Chaucer and the Social Contest*. New York: Routledge, 1990.

Kolve, V. A. *Chaucer and the Imagery of Narrative: The First Five Canterbury Tales*. Stanford: Stanford University Press, 1984.

Kruger, Steven F. *Dreaming in the Middle Ages*. Cambridge: Cambridge University Press, 1992.

Lambert, Mark. "*Troilus,* Books I-III: A Criseydan Reading." In *Essays on* Troilus and Criseyde, ed. Mary Salu, 105–25. Cambridge, England: D. S. Brewer, 1979; rpt. 1982.

Lawlor, John. "The Pattern of Consolation in *The Book of the Duchess.*" In *Chaucer Criticism:* Troilus and Criseyde *and the Minor Poems,* ed. Richard J. Schoeck and Jerome Taylor, 232–60. Notre Dame, Ind.: University of Notre Dame Press, 1961.

Lawton, David. *Chaucer's Narrators.* Suffolk, England: D. S. Brewer, 1985.

Leicester, H. Marshall, Jr. "The Harmony of Chaucer's *Parlement:* A Dissonant Voice." *Chaucer Review* 9 (1974): 15–34.

Leslie, Michael. "An English Landscape Garden before 'The English Landscape Garden'?" *The Journal of Garden History* 13 (1993): 3–15.

Lewis, C. S. "What Chaucer Really Did to *Il Filostrato.*" *Essays and Studies* 17 (1932): 56–75. Rpt. in *Chaucer Criticism,* vol. 2, ed. Richard J. Schoeck and Jerome Taylor, 16–33. Notre Dame, Indiana: University of Notre Dame Press, 1961.

Luttrell, C. A. "*Pearl:* Symbolism in a Garden Setting." *Neophilologus* XLIX (1965): 160–76.

Lynch, Kathryn L. *The High Medieval Dream Vision: Poetry, Philosophy, and Literary Form.* Stanford: Stanford University Press, 1988.

MacDougall, Elisabeth, ed. *Medieval Gardens.* Washington, D.C.: Dumbarton Oaks, 1986.

Macrobius. *Somnium Scipionis,* ed. L. von Jan. Leipzig, 1852. Trans. William Harris Stahl as *Commentary on the Dream of Scipio.* Records of Civilization, Sources and Studies 48. New York: Columbia University Press, 1952.

Magnus, Larry. "The Hem of Philosophy: Free and Bound Motifs in the *Franklin's Tale.*" *Assays* 2 (1982): 3–18.

Manley, John Matthews. "Chaucer and the Rhetoricians." In *Chaucer Criticism:* The Canturbury Tales, ed. Richard J. Schoeck and Jerome Taylor, 268–90. Notre Dame, Ind.: University of Notre Dame Press, 1960.

Marie de France. *Lais,* Ed. Alfred Ewert. Oxford: Blackwell, 1978. Trans. Robert Hanning and Joan Ferrante as *The Lais of Marie de France.* New York: Dutton, 1978.

Martin, Priscilla. *Chaucer's Women: Nun, Wives and Amazons.* London: Macmillan, 1990.

Matter, E. Ann. *The Voice of My Beloved: The Song of Songs in Western Medieval Christianity.* Philadelphia: University of Pennsylvania Press, 1990.

Matthew of Vendôme. "Ars versificatoria." In *Les Arts Poétiques du XIIe et du XIIIe Siècle,* ed. Edmond Faral. Paris: Champion, 1958. 106–93. Trans. Aubrey E. Galyon as *The Art of Versification.* Ames: Iowa State University Press, 1980.

McAlpine, Monica E. *The Genre of* Troilus and Criseyde. Ithaca: Cornell University Press, 1978.

McClellan, William. "Bakhtin's Theory of Dialogic Discourse, Medieval Rhetorical Theory, and the Multi-Voiced Structure of the *Clerk's Tale.*" *Exemplaria* 1.2 (1989): 461–88.

McDonald, Charles O. "An Interpretation of Chaucer's *Parlement of Foules.*" In *Chaucer Criticism:* Troilus and Criseyde *and the Minor Poems,* ed. Richard J. Schoeck and Jerome Taylor, 275–93. Notre Dame, Ind.: University of Notre Dame Press, 1961.
McNamara, Jo Ann, and Suzanne Wemple. "The Power of Women Through the Family in Medieval Europe, 500–1100." In *Women and Power in the Middle Ages,* ed. Mary Erler and Maryanne Kowaleski, 83–101. Athens: University of Georgia Press, 1988.
Mehl, Dieter. *Geoffrey Chaucer: An Introduction to His Narrative Poetry.* Cambridge: Cambridge University Press, 1986.
Meyvaert, Paul. "The Medieval Monastic Garden." In *Medieval Gardens,* ed. Elisabeth B. MacDougall, 25–53. Washington, D.C.: Dumbarton Oaks, 1986.
Murray, Stephen, and James Addiss. "Plan and Space at Amiens Cathedral with a New Plan Drawn by James Addiss." *Journal of the Society of Architectural Historians* 49 (1990): 44–66.
Muscatine, Charles. *Chaucer and the French Tradition: A Study in Style and Meaning.* Berkeley: University of California Press, 1957.
Nolan, Barbara. "The Art of Expropriation: Chaucer's Narrator in Book of the Duchess." In *New Perspectives in Chaucer Criticism,* ed. Donald M. Rose. Norman, Okla.: Pilgrim Books, 1981.
———. *Chaucer and the Tradition of the* Roman *Antique.* Cambridge: Cambridge University Press, 1992.
Ovid. *Metamorphoses,* ed. William S. Anderson. Leipzig: Teubner, 1977.
Payne, Robert O. *The Key of Remembrance: A Study of Chaucer's Poetics.* New Haven: Yale University Press, 1963. Rpt. Westport, Conn.: Greenwood Press, 1973.
Pearl. Ed. E. V. Gordon. Oxford: Clarendon Press, 1990.
Pearsall, Derek, ed. *The Floure and the Leafe, The Assembly of Ladies, The Isle of Ladies.* Kalamazoo, Mich.: Medieval Institute Publications, 1990.
Pearsall, Derek, and Elizabeth Salter. *Landscapes and Seasons of the Medieval World.* London: Paul Elk, 1973.
Phillips, Helen. "Structure and Consolation in the *Book of the Duchess.*" *Chaucer Review* 16 (1981): 107–18.
Piehler, Paul. *The Visionary Landscape: A Study in Medieval Allegory.* London: Edward Arnold, 1971.
Pound, Ezra. *ABC of Reading.* New York: New Directions, 1960.
Power, Eileen. *Medieval Women,* ed. M. M. Postan. Cambridge: Cambridge University Press, 1975.
Pratt, Robert A. "Chaucer's Claudian." *Speculum* 22 (1947): 419–23.
Prior, Sandra Pierson. "*Routhe* and *Hert-Huntyng* in the *Book of the Duchess.*" *JEGP* 85 (1986): 3–19.
Quintilian. *Institutio Oratoria,* trans. H. E. Butler. New York: Putnam's Sons, 1921.

Régnier-Bohler, Danielle. "Imagining the Self." In *A History of Private Life: Revelations of the Medieval World*, vol. 2, ed. Philippe Ariès and Georges Duby, 313–93. Cambridge, Mass.: Belknap Press, 1988.

Robertson, D. W., Jr. "The Book of the Duchess." In *Companion to Chaucer Studies*, ed. Beryl Rowland, 332–40. London: Oxford University Press, 1968.

———. "The Doctrine of Charity in Medieval Literary Gardens: A Topical Approach through Symbolism and Allegory." *Speculum* 26 (1951): 24–49. Rpt. in *Essays in Medieval Culture*, 21–50. Princeton: Princeton University Press, 1980.

Rudat, Wolfgang E.H. "Gentillesse and the Marriage Debate in the *Franklin's Tale*: Chaucer's Squires and the Question of Nobility." *Neophilologus* 68 (1984): 451–70.

Russell, J. Stephen. *The English Dream Vision: Anatomy of a Form*. Columbus: Ohio State University Press, 1988.

Salter, Elizabeth. "*Troilus and Criseyde:* Poet and Narrator." In *Acts of Interpretation*, ed. Mary Carruthers and Elizabeth Kirk. Norman, Okla.: Pilgrim Books, 1982.

Schildgen, Brenda Deen. "Dante's Utopian Landscape: The Garden of God." In *The Medieval World of Nature*, ed. Joyce E. Salisbury, 201–19. New York: Garland Press, 1993.

Schless, Howard R. *Chaucer and Dante: A Revaluation*. Norman, Okla.: Pilgrim Books, 1984.

Severs, J. Burke. "Chaucer's Self-Portrait in the *Book of the Duchess*." *Philological Quarterly* 43 (1964): 27–39.

Shoaf, R. A. "The *Franklin's Tale:* Chaucer and Medusa." *Chaucer Review* 21 (1986): 274–90.

———. "Notes Toward Chaucer's Poetics of Translation." *Studies in the Age of Chaucer* 1 (1979): 55–66.

———. "Stalking the Sorrowful H(e)art: Penitential Lore and the Hunt Scene in Chaucer's *The Book of the Duchess*." *JEGP* 78 (1979): 313–24.

Smith, Nathaniel B. "In Search of the Ideal Landscape: From 'Locus Amoenus' to 'Parc du champ joli' in the 'Roman de la Rose.'" *Viator* 11 (1980): 225–43.

Smyser, H. M. "The Domestic Background of *Troilus and Criseyde*." *Speculum* 31 (1956): 297–315.

Spearing, A. C. *Medieval Dream-Poetry*. Cambridge: Cambridge University Press, 1976.

Statius. "Epithalamion in Stellam et Violentillam." In *Silvae* I.ii, ed. E. Courtney, 6–15. Oxford: Clarendon Press, 1990. Trans. J. H. Mozley as "An Epithalamium in Honour of Stella and Violentilla," in *Silvae*, 15–37. New York: G. P. Putnam's Sons: 1928.

———. *Thebaid*, ed. and trans. J. H. Mozley. Cambridge: Harvard University Press, 1928; rpt. 1955, 1957.

Stewart, Stanley. *The Enclosed Garden: The Tradition and the Image in Seventeenth-Century Poetry.* Madison: University of Wisconsin Press, 1966.
Stock, Lorraine Kochanske. "The Two Mayings in Chaucer's *Knight's Tale:* Convention and Invention." *JEGP* 85 (1986): 206–21.
Taylor, Karla. *Chaucer Reads "The Divine Comedy."* Stanford: Stanford University Press, 1989.
———. "Inferno 5 and *Troilus and Criseyde* Revisited." In *Chaucer's* Troilus and Criseyde: *"Subgit to Alle Poesye,"* ed. R. A. Shoaf, 239–56. Binghamton, N.Y.: Medieval and Renaissance Texts and Studies, 1992.
Thornton, Gladys A. *A History of Clare, Suffolk.* Cambridge: W. Heffer and Sons, 1928.
Underhill, Frances A. "Elizabeth de Burgh: Connoisseur and Patron." In *The Cultural Patronage of Medieval Women,* ed. June Hall McCash, 266–87. Athens: University of Georgia Press, 1996.
van Buren, Anne Hagopian. "Reality and Literary Romance in the Park of Hesdin." In *Medieval Gardens,* ed. Elisabeth B. MacDougall. Washington, D.C.: Dumbarton Oaks, 1986.
Vance, Eugene. *Mervelous Signals: Poetics and Sign Theory in the Middle Ages.* Lincoln: University of Nebraska Press, 1986.
Von Kreisler, Nicolai. "The *Locus Amoenus* and Eschatological Lore in the *Parliament of Fowls* 204–10." *Philological Quarterly* 50 (1971): 16–22.
Walker, Denis. "Narrative Inconclusiveness and Consolatory Dialectic in the *Book of the Duchess.*" *Chaucer Review* 18 (1983): 1–17.
Wallace, David. *Chaucer and the Early Writings of Boccaccio.* Bury St. Edmunds, England: D. S. Brewer, 1985.
Walsh, P. G., ed. and trans. *Andreas Capellanus on Love.* London: Duckworth, 1982.
Waswo, Richard. "The Narrator of *Troilus and Criseyde.*" *ELH* 50 (1983): 1–25.
Wetherbee, Winthrop. *Chaucer: The Canterbury Tales.* Cambridge: Cambridge University Press, 1989.
———. *Chaucer and the Poets: An Essay on* Troilus and Criseyde. Ithaca: Cornell University Press, 1984.
Wimsatt, James I. "The French Element in *Troilus and Criseyde.*" *Yearbook of English Studies* 15 (1985): 18–32.
———. "Guillaume de Machaut and Chaucer's *Troilus and Criseyde.*" *Medium Aevum* 45 (1976): 277–93.
———. *The Marguerite Poetry of Guillaume de Machaut.* Studies in the Romance Languages and Literatures, vol. 87. Chapel Hill: University of North Carolina Press, 1970.
Windeatt, Barry A. "Chaucer and the *Filostrato.*" In *Chaucer and the Italian Trecento,* ed. Piero Boitani, 163–83. Cambridge: Cambridge University Press, 1983.

———, ed. and trans. *Chaucer's Dream Poetry: Sources and Analogues.* London: D. S. Brewer, 1982.
———. "Love That Oughte Ben Secree." *Chaucer Review* 14 (1979): 116–31.
———. *Oxford Guides to Chaucer:* Troilus and Criseyde. Oxford: Clarendon Press, 1992.
———. "'Troilus' and the Disenchantment of Romance." In *Studies in Medieval English Romances: Some New Approaches,* ed. Derek Brewer, 129–47. Cambridge: D. S. Brewer, 1988.
Woods, Marjorie Curry, ed. *An Early Commentary on the* Poetria nova *of Geoffrey of Vinsauf.* New York: Garland Press, 1985.
Woods, William F. "Chivalry and Nature in *The Knight's Tale.*" *Philological Quarterly* 66 (1987): 287–301.

Index

Adam, 101
Addiss, James, 26
Aers, David, 120n.16, 123n.28
Affricanus, 62
Agape, 96–97
Albertus Magnus, 22–24
Alcione. *See* Ceyx and Alcione
Amiens Cathedral, 26
Amplificatio, 16
Andreas Capellanus, 6–7, 65, 76, 78, 105–6, 109
Antenor, 67
Antigone, 66, 71–73, 79
Appleton, Jay, 112n.24
Arcite, 87–92, 122n.20
Argus, 44, 49
Arthurian legend, 28–29, 79; and Lady of the Lake, 23
Arveragus, 102–9, 124n.36
Assembly of Ladies, The, 3
Athena. *See* Pallas Athena
Auctoritas, 35–36
Augustine, St. (of Hippo), 197
Aurelius, 104–9, 124n.36

Bakhtin, Mikhail, 86–87, 121nn.8, 9
Barney, Stephen A., 117n.34
Bennett, J. A. W., 118n.49
Bennett, Judith M., 85
Benton, John F., 120n.2
Birdsong, 16–17, 117n.36; in *Book of the Duchess*, 39, 51; in *Parliament of Fowls*, 58

Black Knight, The, 37–39, 41–43, 49, 51–53
Bleeth, Kenneth A., 123n.32
Boccaccio, Giovanni, 10; *Ameto*, 96–97; *Amorosa visione*, 118n.47; *Decameron*, 23; *Filocolo*, 69, 108, 124n.36; *Filostrato*, 65–68, 74–76, 82, 90 (Fig. 6), 119n.12, 122n.16; *Teseida*, 56, 57–60, 90–91
Bodiam Castle (Sussex), 5, 23, 28–29
Boethius, 77–78, 87
Book of the Duchess, 3, 12, 15, 35–55, 62
Borthwick, Mary Charlotte, 120nn.18, 19
Bridle, 77–78
Burlin, Robert M., 116n.20
Burnley, J. D., 121n.11

Calin, William, 118n.59, 123n.27
Calkas, 78–79
Calkins, Robert, 24
Carruthers, Mary, 21
Catalogue of trees, 10, 19–20, 99; and mixed forests, 23; in *Parliament of Fowls*, 57, 61. *See also* Trees
Ceyx and Alcione, 38, 40, 42, 51
Charles V, King of France, 24
Charles VI, King of France, 24
Chaucer, Geoffrey: and dream-poems, 9–10; French influence on, 5, 15–16, 35–36, 44–49, 55–58, 65–66, 96–97, 123n.27; Italian influence on, 58–59,

Chaucer—*Continued*
  65–68, 74–76, 96–97; and relations to literary predecessors, 2–3, 11, 21, 52, 62–64, 80–82. *See also* individual works
Chrétien de Troyes, 79
Christine de Pizan, 32 (Fig. 3), 34
Clare Castle (Suffolk), 29, 30–31, 114n.62
Claudian, 18, 19, 98
Clemen, Wolfgang, 115n.5
Coleman, Janet, 48
Colvin, Howard, 25, 29
Comito, Terry, 4
Commonplaces. *See* Loci communes
Convention, 2, 11–13, 52–54, 62–63; and *Book of the Duchess*, 38, 48, 53; and *Canterbury Tales*, 83–84, 109; and courtly love, 66, 69–72, 76; and genre, 11, 52; and humor, 49; and misogyny, 87; and narrative, 36, 53, 109; and *Parliament of Fowls*, 61–62; and *Troilus and Criseyde*, 80–82. *See also* Rhetoric; Topoi
Cosgrove, Denis, 112n.24
Court of Love, 7–8. *See also* Love
Crane, Susan, 88, 91, 122nn.16, 17, 21
Creon, 89, 94
Crescenzi, Piero de', 23–24, 43–44, 45 (Fig. 5)
Criseyde, 64–82, 86, 119n.15, 120n.24, 121nn.32, 33, 11
Cupid, 99
Curtius, Ernst Robert, 16, 20, 21
Cyane, 98
Cytherea, 54, 61, 118n.49. *See also* Venus

Dalyngrigge, Sir Edward, 28
Damyan, 100–101
Dante, 9–10, 34, 43, 118nn.47, 49; and *Parliament of Fowls*, 56, 60–61
De Certeau, Michel, 9, 27, 52
Deiphebus, 73–74, 76, 79
Deschamps, Eustache, 5; *Le lay de Franchise*, 114n.70; *Miroir de Mariage*, 96
Diamond, Arlyn, 120n.31, 121n.12
Diana, 92–94, 99, 122n.16

Dido, 80
Diomedes, 78
Dodd, William George, 120n.25
Donaldson, E. Talbot, 122n.14
Dorigen, 102–9, 124nn.36, 37, 42
Dream-poems, 36–37, 51–53, 54–55, 62–63, 80
Duby, Georges, 85, 120n.16, 121n.6, 124n.43

Earthly paradise, 10, 33 (Fig. 4); and *Franklin's Tale*, 103; and *Knight's Tale*, 88; and *locus amoenus*, 16–19; and *Merchant's Tale*, 95, 101; and *Parliament of Fowls*, 56–60; and Renaissance gardens, 4
Eckhardt, Caroline D., 116n.28
Economou, George D., 119n.2
Eden, 101. *See also* Earthly paradise
Elizabeth de Burgh (the elder, Lady of Clare), 30
Elizabeth de Burgh (the younger, Countess of Ulster), 30, 114n.62
Emelye, 20, 87–94, 95, 122nn.13, 14, 20
Engle, Lars, 121n.8
Eve, 101, 102, 123n.32
Everett, Dorothy, 115n.14
Fabliau, 123n.33
Ferrante, Joan M., 79, 119n.2, 120n.31, 121n.7
Ferster, Judith, 118n.55, 124n.36
Fields, 84, 91
Fishponds, 24, 25, 30. *See also* Pools; Wells
Flora, 44, 46–48
Floure and the Leafe, The, 3
Flowers: in *Book of the Duchess*, 46–48; in built gardens, 24, 25; in *Knight's Tale*, 91; in manuscript illumination, 34, 90; in *Merchant's Tale*, 95; in *Parliament of Fowls*, 58; in rhetorical treatises, 16–18. *See also* Fragrance
Fountains, 22, 27 (Fig. 1), 28; at Clare Castle, 30; and courtly love, 66, 68; at Park of Hesdin, 25–26
Fragrance, 17, 20, 104. *See also* Flowers

Franc Vouloir, 96–97
Frank, Robert Worth, Jr., 62, 117n.44
Franklin's Tale, 12, 19, 83, 102–9
Free will, 93
Froissart, Jean, 10, 15, 35, 58; "Le Cour de May," 118n.47; *Le Paradys d'Amours,* 69, 118n.51
Fyler, John M., 115n.8, 119n.14, 124n.35

Ganim, John M., 121nn.8, 9, 123n.34
Garden(s): activity in, 33–34, 66, 69, 103; animals in, 23, 24, 30, 44, 49, 58; and antigarden, 84; Arveragus's, 103; buildings in, 23–25, 29–30; Criseyde's, 3, 70–71, 73, 103; Deiphebus's, 73–74; design of, 22–24, 29, 31; and distance from residence, 5, 24, 29; eavesdropping in, 34; enclosed, 4–5, 19, 24, 31 (Fig. 2), 55–56, 65, 69, 84, 88, 89, 97; entrance into, 36, 55–56, 60; January's, 1–2, 99–102, 123nn.31, 32; manuscript illumination of, 27 (Fig. 1), 31 (Fig. 2), 32 (Fig. 3), 45 (Fig. 5), 90 (Fig. 6); metaphorical uses of, 5–6, 11, 53–54, 62–63, 69–70; monastic, 31–33; negative aspects of, 19, 58–60, 83–84; painting of, 33 (Fig. 4); for pleasure, 5, 22, 23–34, 27 (Fig. 1), 43–44, 66, 73–74, 91, 97, 99, 103; as prisons, 87–89, 122n.13; real and imagined, 22, 23, 29–30, 58, 71; in Renaissance, 4, 5; as rhetorical *topoi,* 10, 21–22; royal, 22, 23, 24–26, 29–30; sex in, 1–2; Theseus's, 87–88, 94; and Troilus, 68–70, 77; and wives, 83–87. *See also* Birdsong; Catalogue of trees; Earthly paradise; Fishponds; Flowers; Fountains; Fragrance; *Hortus conclusus; Hortus deliciarum; Locus amoenus;* Mazes; Moats; Outdoor rooms; *Paradys d'amours;* Pools; Privacy; Shade; Trees; Turf benches; Walls; Wells; Woods
Garden of Déduit, 15, 18–19, 20, 60, 123n.26
Garden of Love. *See Paradys d'amours*
Gender: roles, 84–85; and power 84–86, 97–99

Genre, 11, 13, 52, 88. *See also* Romance
Geoffrey of Vinsauf, 6, 8, 62–63, 116n.16; and *Book of the Duchess,* 43, 46, 49–51; and narrative structure, 39
Giamatti, A. Bartlett, 4, 17, 18, 112n.6
Giovanni di Paolo di Grazia, 33 (Fig. 4), 34
God of Love, 69. *See also* Love
Gordon, Ida, 120n.18
Guildford manor, 22
Guillaume de Lorris, 15, 18–19, 20, 44–46, 56. *See also* Jean de Meun; *Roman de la Rose*
Guillaume de Machaut, 10, 15, 35, 63, 123n.27; and *Book of the Duchess,* 38; and *Parliament of Fowls,* 58; Works: *Le Dit de la Fonteinne Amoureuse,* 118n.51; *Le Dit dou Lyon,* 115n.9; *Le Jugement dou Roy de Behaingne,* 114n.70; *Mireoir amoureux,* 71; *Le Paradis d'Amour,* 71; *Remède de Fortune,* 5, 23

Hallissy, Margaret, 119n.15
Hanning, Robert W., 118n.59, 121nn.7, 34, 122nn.13, 17
Hansen, Elaine Tuttle, 122n.12
Harrison, Benjamin S., 115n.14
Harvey, John H., 5, 24, 25, 32, 113n.33
Heffernan, Carol Falvo, 117n.46, 124n.36
Helen of Troy, 73–74, 76–79, 120n.24
Henry I, King of England, 24
Henry II, King of England, 23, 29–30
Henry III, King of England, 22
Henry V, King of England, 25
Homer, 16
Hortus conclusus, 10, 19; and *Knight's Tale,* 88; and *Merchant's Tale,* 110, 102; and *Parliament of Fowls,* 35, 55–56
Hortus deliciarum, 19, 60
Howard, Donald R., 48, 122nn.17, 21
Hundred Years' War, 48
Huppé, Bernard, 43

Invenio, 115n.70
Isidore of Seville, 18

Jacobs, Kathryn, 124n.35
January (of the *Merchant's Tale*), 1–2, 95–102
Jauss, Hans Robert, 11
Jean de Meun, 15, 19, 46–48, 60. *See also* Guillaume de Lorris; *Roman de la Rose*
Jerusalem, 56
Jewels, 17–18, 56
"Johannes," 31 (Fig. 2)
John of Gaunt, 29, 31
Jordan, Robert M., 116n.7
Joseph of Exeter, 19
Journey, 6, 8, 9–10, 26–28. *See also* Walking
Jove, 99
Justinus, 95, 102

Kaske, Robert E., 123n.31
Kee, Kenneth, 113n.19, 123n.31, 124n.36
Kelley, Michael R., 117n.44
Kellogg, Alfred L., 123n.31
Kelly, Douglas, 115n.14
Kenilworth Castle, 25
Kiser, Lisa, 52, 115n.8, 117n.32, 120n.18
Kittredge, G. L., 102, 124n.35
Knapp, Peggy, 121n.8
Knight's Tale, 12, 20, 83, 87–95
Kolve, V. A., 87, 114n.70, 122nn.13, 18
Kruger, Steven, 36–37

Lambert, Mark, 121n.11
Lawlor, John, 115n.8
Lawton, David, 63, 116n.27
Leicester, H. Marshall, Jr., 35, 55, 117nn.38, 46, 118nn.50, 55
Leslie, Michael, 5, 28
Lewis, C. S., 65
Lionel, Duke of Clarence, 30
Loci communes, 21
Locus amoenus, 10, 35; as abode of Venus, 18; and *Parliament of Fowls*, 48, 59, 62; as *topos*, 16–18; and *Troilus and Criseyde*, 71–71, 99
Love: courtly, 64, 65, 69–70, 71–82, 89, 104–5, 109; and Criseyde, 70–73; as game, 107; in poetry, 18–19; secrecy in, 65, 76–80, 120n.25; and Troilus, 68–70. *See also* Andreas Capellanus; Court of Love; Cytherea; God of Love; Venus
Luttrell, C. A., 112n.13
Lying, 107
Lynch, Kathryn, 53
Lyric: Antigone's song, 71–73, 120n.18; Boethius' II. metrum 8, 77–78; Hymn to Venus, 74–76; and narrative, 36, 79; in *Troilus and Criseyde*, 66, 68, 69–70

Macrobius, 54, 62. *See also* Dream-poems
Magnus, Larry, 124n.44
Malory, Sir Thomas, 79
"Man in black." *See* Black Knight
Manley, John M. 115n.14
Marie de France, 52, 79, 80
Marriage, 84–85, 124n.43; in *Franklin's Tale*, 104–5, 107–8, 124n.36; in *Knight's Tale* 89, 92–93; in *Merchant's Tale*, 95–96, 99–102; in *Troilus and Criseyde*, 68, 77–78
Marriage group, 102, 124n.35
Mars, 74–75, 93
Martin, Priscilla, 83, 108, 121n.1, 122n.21, 124n.45
Mary, St. *See* Virgin Mary
Matthew of Vendôme, 16
May: observance of, 88, 91–92, 122n.20
May (of *Merchant's Tale*), 1–2, 95–102
Mazes, 3, 24, 29
McAlpine, Monica E., 120n.24
McClellan, William, 121n.8
McDonald, Charles O., 117n.46
McNamara, Jo Ann, 84
Mehl, Dieter, 53, 115n.5
Memory, 21–22
Merchant's Tale, 1, 12, 19–20, 83, 95–102
Misogyny, 87, 93
Moats, 25, 30, 32
Mortimer, Roger, 30
Murray, Stephen, 26
Muscatine, Charles, 37, 64, 69

Narrative, 52; artificial vs. natural, 39–40, 42–43, 49–53, 115n.14; and chivalry, 92; chronology, 50–51; convention, 36,

52–53, 109; and courtly love, 102; and dialogic discourse, 86–87; incoherent, 37, 54; lyriclike, 51, 53. *See also* Tale
Nationalism, 48
Nature, in *Parliament of Fowls*, 55, 62, 63
Nolan, Barbara, 52

Occupatio, 89
Octavian, 39
Outdoor rooms, 10, 30
Ovid, 10, 19, 82, 98

Palamon, 87–92, 122n.20
Pallas Athena, 99
Paradys d'amours, 10, 49, 113n.19; in *Book of the Duchess*, 35, 43–44, 52, 53; and the earthly paradise, 4; in *Franklin's Tale*, 103, 108; and French poetry, 15, 16, 18, 20; in *Merchant's Tale*, 97–100, 102; in *Parliament of Fowls*, 55, 57, 61–62; in *Troilus and Criseyde*, 66, 69, 70, 72, 78, 82; walking in, 6. *See also* Gardens; Love
Pandarus, 68–70, 73, 77
Park. *See* Woods
Park of Hesdin (Artois), 5, 23, 25–28
Parliament of Fowls, 12, 15, 35, 49, 54–63
Paths, 6, 24, 27 (Fig. 1); of art, 8, 39–40, 49; at Clare Castle, 30; in Criseyde's garden, 71; in *De Amore*, 6–8; as metaphors, 6-10; of nature, 8, 39–40, 49; at Park of Hesdin, 27–28
Payne, Robert O., 65
Pearl, 17–18
Pearsall, Derek, 5, 16, 23
Peterborough Abbey, 32
Petronius, 16
Piehler, Paul, 5
Piramus, 79–80
Pluto, 97–99, 102, 123n.29
Pools, 29. *See also* Fishponds; Wells
Power, Eileen, 84
Priapus, 97, 99
Privacy, 32 (Fig. 3), 73, 88, 103. *See also* Walls, surrounding gardens
Proserpine, 97–100, 101–2, 123n.29
Prudentius, 17

Queynte, 123n.22
Quintilian, M. Fabius, 20, 113n.25

Radbertus, Paschasius, abbot of Corbie, 19
Repertoire de Science, 96
Retraction, 55
Revelation, 56
Rhetoric, 21, 115n.14. *See also* *Amplificatio*; Catalogue of trees; *Invenio*; *Occupatio*; *Topoi*
Robert II, Count of Artois, 25. *See also* Park of Hesdin
Robertson, D. W., 10–11, 43, 115n.10, 123n.31
Romance, 69, 79, 88, 121n.32. *See also* Genre
Roman d'Aneas, 80
Roman de la Rose, 4, 5, 18, 27 (Fig. 1), 28, 35; and *Book of the Duchess*, 41, 44, 49, 51–52, 53; and *Merchant's Tale*, 97–98, 101, 123n.26; and Park of Hesdin, 23, 26, 27; and *Parliament of Fowls*, 55–56, 57, 58, 118n.47; and *Troilus and Criseyde*, 69; two gardens in, 15–16
Roman de Thèbes, 79
Roman de Troie, 79
Rosamund's Bower. *See* Henry II, King of England
Rudat, Wolfgang, 124n.44
Rupert of Deutz, 19

Salter, Elizabeth, 5, 16, 23
Schildgen, Brenda Deen, 118n.47
Schless, Howard R., 118n.47
Secrecy. *See* Privacy
Sedes, 21; *argumentorum*, 20
Shade: in *Book of the Duchess*, 43; in garden treatises, 22, 24; in *locus amoenus*, 16–17; in *paradys d'amours*, 20; in *Parliament of Fowls*, 56; as positive feature, 43, 116n.22; in *Troilus and Criseyde*, 70. *See also* Trees; Woods
Shoaf, R. A., 35, 53, 124n.42
Smyser, H. M., 119n.5
Song. *See* Lyric
Song of Songs, 10, 123n.30; and *Knight's Tale*, 88, 92; and *Merchant's Tale*, 100–

101; and *Parliament of Fowls*, 56; and Virgin Mary, 19
Spearing, A. C., 115n.12, 116n.32
Statius, 18, 19
Stewart, Stanley, 4
Stock, Lorraine Kochanske, 122nn.20, 21, 14, 16
Streams, 16, 17

Tale, 40–43, 54, 117n.34. *See also* Narrative
Taylor, Karla, 64, 121n.32
Tertullian, 17
Theocritus, 16
Theophrastus, 95
Theseus, 87–94
Thisbe, 79–80
Thornton, Gladys, 30
Tiberianus, 16
Topoi, 20–21; and *Book of the Duchess*, 37, 53; and *Canterbury Tales*, 83; and garden design, 22–23; and *Merchant's Tale*, 97, 102; and *Parliament of Fowls*, 57, 62; and poetic tradition, 35, 48–49; and *Troilus and Criseyde*, 83. *See also* Rhetoric
Trees: in *Book of the Duchess*, 38, 43; in earthly paradise, 17; with fruit, 17, 20, 23, 24, 25, 29, 34; in *locus amoenus*, 16, 17; in *Merchant's Tale*, 95; in *Parliament of Fowls*, 56; in pleasure gardens, 22; in *Wife of Bath's Prologue*, 83–84. *See also* Catalogue of trees; Shade
Tristan and Isolde, 23, 29–30, 79
Troilus, 64–82
Troilus and Criseyde, 3, 12, 42, 64–82
Trouthe, 107
Turf benches, 3, 90 (Fig. 6); and courtly love, 66, 68; in Criseyde's garden, 70, 71; in ideal pleasure garden, 22

Van Buren, Anne Hagopian, 5, 25
Vance, Eugene, 107, 119n.6

Venus, 63, 66–67, 88, 93, 98–99, 122n.16; abode of, 15, 18; hymn to, 74–76; Temple of, 54, 55, 58, 62, 63. *See also* Cytherea
Virgil, 10, 16
Virgin Mary, 19, 92, 123n.32
Von Kreisler, Nicolai, 118n.48

Walker, Denis, 116n.8
Walking, 6, 8–9, 11, 28, 30, 52. *See also* Journey
Wallace, David, 65
Walls, surrounding gardens: in manuscript illuminations, 27 (Fig. 1), 31 (Fig. 2), 34; in *Merchant's Tale*, 97; at Park of Hesdin, 25; in *Parliament of Fowls*, 55; at Peterborough Abbey, 32; recommended by Crescenzi, 23; in *Troilus and Criseyde*, 73; at Windsor Castle, 25. *See also* Gardens, enclosed
Wells, 69, 97. *See also* Fishponds; Fountains; Pools
Wemple, Suzanne, 84
Wetherbee, Winthrop, 119n.3, 123n.29
Wife of Bath's Prologue and Tale, 83–84, 96, 101, 123n.31
Wilderness, 43, 84
Wimsatt, James I., 119n.6
Winchester Cathedral Priory, 32
Windeatt, B. A., 64, 65, 69, 119n.3, 121nn.5, 10, 120n.25
Windsor Castle, 24–25
Woods, 45 (Fig. 5); in *Book of the Duchess*, 43–44; in Park of Hesdin, 25–26. *See also* Shade; Trees
Woods, Marjorie Curry, 116n.16
Woods, William, 122n.14

Ypolita, 88

Zephirus, 18, 44, 46–48

OHIO UNIVERSITY LIBRARY

Please return this book as soon as you have finished with it. In order to avoid a fine it must be returned by the latest date stamped below. All books are subject to recall after two weeks or immediately if needed for reserve.

JUN 1 6 2001   JUN 1 5 2001

CF